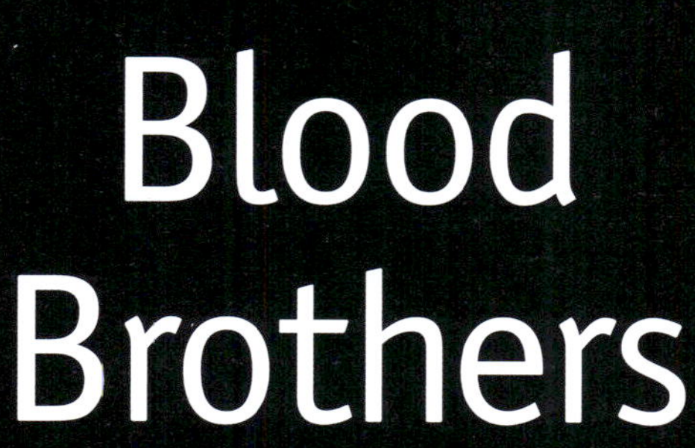

Blood Brothers

by Willy Russell

Kevin Radford

Series Editors:
Sue Bennett and Dave Stockwin

The Publishers would like to thank the following for permission to reproduce copyright material.

Photo credits

p. 8 TopFoto; **p. 10** jeremy sutton-hibbert/Alamy; **p. 12** TopFoto; **p. 17** Photostage; **p. 27** Trinity Mirror/Mirrorpix/Alamy; **p. 50** Glasshouse Images/Alamy; **p. 52** Fotolia; **p. 55** Trinity Mirror/Mirrorpix/Alamy; **p. 60** Homer Sykes Archive/Alamy.

Acknowledgements

Extracts from the play: © Willy Russell, 2009, *Blood Brothers*, Bloomsbury Methuen Drama, used by permission of Bloomsbury Publishing Plc.

Every effort has been made to trace all copyright holders, but if any have been inadvertently overlooked, the Publishers will be pleased to make the necessary arrangements at the first opportunity.

Although every effort has been made to ensure that website addresses are correct at time of going to press, Hodder Education cannot be held responsible for the content of any website mentioned in this book. It is sometimes possible to find a relocated web page by typing in the address of the home page for a website in the URL window of your browser.

Hachette UK's policy is to use papers that are natural, renewable and recyclable products and made from wood grown in sustainable forests. The logging and manufacturing processes are expected to conform to the environmental regulations of the country of origin.

Orders: please contact Bookpoint Ltd, 130 Park Drive, Milton Park, Abingdon, Oxon OX14 4SE. Telephone: (44) 01235 827720. Fax: (44) 01235 400454. Email education@bookpoint.co.uk Lines are open from 9 a.m. to 5 p.m., Monday to Saturday, with a 24-hour message answering service. You can also order through our website: www.hoddereducation.co.uk

ISBN: 978 1 4718 5357 9

First published in 2016 by

Hodder Education,

An Hachette UK Company

Carmelite House

50 Victoria Embankment

London EC4Y 0DZ

www.hoddereducation.co.uk

Impression number 10 9 8 7 6 5 4 3 2 1

Year 2020 2019 2018 2017 2016

Cover photo © Jane1e/iStock/Thinkstock/Getty Images

Typeset in 11/13pt Bliss Light by Integra Software Services Pvt. Ltd., Pondicherry, India

Printed in Italy

A catalogue record for this title is available from the British Library.

Contents

Getting the most from this guide

This guide is designed to help you raise your achievement in your examination response to *Blood Brothers*. It is intended for you to use throughout your GCSE English literature course: it will help you when you are studying the play for the first time and also during your revision.

The following features have been used throughout this guide to help you focus your understanding of the play.

Target your thinking

A list of **introductory questions**, labelled by Assessment Objective, is provided at the beginning of each chapter to give you a breakdown of the material covered. These questions target your thinking, in order to help you work more efficiently by focusing on the key messages.

Build critical skills

These boxes offer an opportunity to consider some **more challenging questions**. They are designed to encourage deeper thinking, analysis and exploratory thought. Building and practising critical skills in this way will give you a real advantage in the examination.

GRADE *FOCUS*

It is possible to know a play well and yet still underachieve in the examination if you are unsure what the examiners are looking for. These boxes give a clear explanation of **how you may be assessed**, with an emphasis on the criteria for gaining a Grade 5 and a Grade 8.

REVIEW YOUR LEARNING

At the end of each chapter you will find this section to **test your knowledge**: it provides a series of short, specific questions to ensure that you have understood and absorbed the key messages of the chapter. Answers to the 'Review your learning' questions are provided in the final section of the guide (pages 98–100).

GRADE *BOOSTER*

Read and remember these pieces of helpful **grade-boosting advice**. They provide top tips from experienced teachers and examiners who can advise you on what to do, as well as what *not* to do, in order to maximise your chances of success in the examination.

Key quotation

Key quotations are highlighted for you, so that if you wish you may use them as **supporting evidence** in your examination answers. Further quotations, grouped by characterisation and theme, can be found in the 'Top quotations' section of the guide (pages 94–96). All page references in this study guide are to the 2009 Bloomsbury Methuen Drama edition of *Blood Brothers* (ISBN 978-0-4137-6770-7).

Mickey: *Well, how come you got everything ... an' I got nothin'?*
(Page 105)

Introduction

Studying the text

You may find it useful to dip into this guide in sections as and when you need them, rather than reading it from start to finish. For example, the section on 'Context' can be read before you read the play itself, since it offers an explanation of the relevant historical, cultural and literary background to the text. In 'Context' you will find information about aspects of Russell's life and times that influenced his writing, the particular issues with which Russell was concerned and where the play stands in terms of the literary tradition to which it belongs.

The relevant 'Plot and structure' sections in this guide may be helpful to you either before or after you read each section of *Blood Brothers*. It combines a summary of events with a commentary, so that you are aware of both the key events and the literary features in each section of the play. The chapters on 'Characterisation', 'Themes' and 'Language, style and analysis' will help develop your thinking further, in preparation for written responses on particular aspects of the text.

Many students also enjoy the experience of being able to bring something extra to their classroom lessons in order to be 'a step ahead of the game'. Alternatively, you may have missed a classroom session or feel that you need a clearer explanation. The guide can help with this, too.

An initial reading of the chapter on 'Assessment Objectives and skills' will enable you to make really effective notes in preparation for your written answers, because you will have a very clear understanding of what the examiners are looking for. The Assessment Objectives are what examination boards base their mark schemes on, and in this section they are broken down and clearly explained.

Revising the text

Whether you study the play in a block of time close to the exam or much earlier in your GCSE English literature course, you will need to revise thoroughly if you are to achieve the very best grade you can.

Reading this guide should, of course, never be a substitute for reading *Blood Brothers* itself, but it can help. You should first remind yourself of what happens in the play, and for this the chapter on 'Plot and structure' might be revisited in the first instance. You might then look at the 'Assessment Objectives and skills' section to ensure you understand what the examiners are, in general, looking for.

'Tackling the exams' then gives you useful information on the exams and question format, depending on which examination board specification you are following, as well as advice on the examination format and practical considerations such as the time available for the question and the Assessment Objectives that apply to it. Advice is also supplied on how to approach the question and on writing a quick plan. All of the examination boards except WJEC Eduqas use a traditional essay-style question for *Blood Brothers*; WJEC Eduqas uses an extract-based question. Focused advice on how you might improve your grade follows, and you need to read this section carefully.

You will find examples of exam-style responses in the 'Sample essays' section, with an examiner's comments in the margins so that you can see clearly how to move towards a Grade 5, and how then to move from a Grade 5 to a Grade 8. When looking at the sample answers, bear in mind that the way they are assessed is similar (but not identical) across the boards. It is sensible to look online at the sample questions and materials from the particular board that you are taking, and to try planning answers to as many questions as possible. You might also have fun inventing and answering additional questions, since you can be sure that the ones in the sample materials will not be the ones you see when you open the exam paper!

This guide should help you clarify your thinking about the play, but it is not a substitute for your own thoughtful reading and discussion of *Blood Brothers*. The guide should also help you consolidate your approach to writing well under the pressure of the examination. The suggestions in the guide can help you develop habits of planning and writing answers that take the worry out of *how* you write, and so enable you to concentrate on *what* you write.

The guide is intended to complement the work you do with your teacher, not to replace it. At the end of the main sections there are 'Review your learning' questions to support your thinking. There are 'Build critical skills' and 'Grade booster' boxes at various points; these will help you develop the critical and analytical skills you need to achieve a higher grade. Now that all GCSE literature examinations are 'closed book', the 'Top quotations' section will prove helpful in offering you the opportunity to learn short quotations to support points about characters and themes, as well as being a revision aid.

When writing about the play, use this guide as a springboard to develop your own ideas. You should not read this guide in order to memorise chunks of it, ready to regurgitate in the exam. Examiners are not looking for set responses; identical answers are dull. They would like to see that you have used everything you have been taught – including by this guide – as a starting point for your own

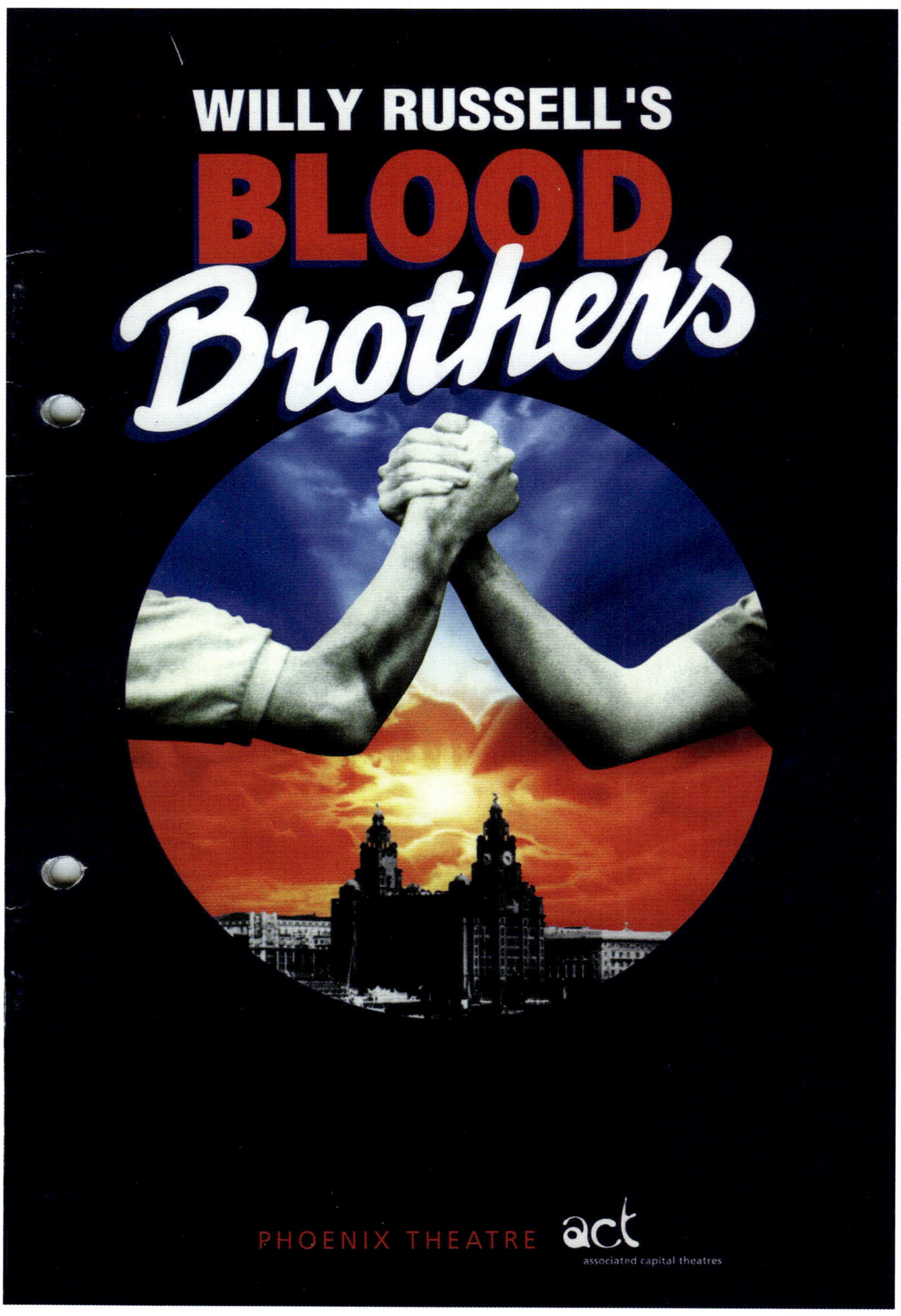

▲ A poster advertising *Blood Brothers*

thinking. The examiners hope to reward you for perceptive thought, individual appreciation and varying interpretations. Try to show that you have engaged with the themes and ideas in the play and that you have explored Russell's methods with an awareness of the context in which he wrote. Above all, don't be afraid to make it clear that you have enjoyed this part of your literature course.

Approaching the play text

A play is, above all, a narrative. A large part of the dramatist's art is to make you want to find out what happens next, and therefore to keep you watching or reading to the end. In order to study *Blood Brothers* and enjoy it, you need to keep a close eye on the events that take place but also to consider the effects that Russell uses to keep his audience engaged.

You also need to keep track of a number of other features that are part of what is called the 'performance context', for example how Russell uses the different settings in his play, what the characters' motivations are and how these are revealed in, say, stage directions. If you watch a stage production, consider how characters are presented differently in this. Further considerations for a drama text rather than a novel include the importance of costume, props and lighting.

Film and stage productions

Stage productions of *Blood Brothers* do exist, so it would be beneficial for you to keep an eye out for any local or national companies staging a production. Remember, plays are written to be performed on stage and not just to be read in a book. Valuable insights may be gained into character and motivation by seeing characters 'come to life' on stage. Seeing the effect of the stage directions, the stage lighting and also the costumes worn, can enhance your understanding of the play.

Blood Brothers is one of Russell's most popular plays and has stood the test of time – people see it as being as relevant today as when it was written. It is still one of the most popular British musicals. As well as live stage productions, you might want to check out the variety of clips of the play that exist on YouTube.

Enjoy referring to the guide as you study the text, and good luck in your exam.

Context

Target your thinking

- What is meant by 'context'? (**AO3**)
- What does the context of the play tell us about its purpose? (**AO3**)
- How did Russell's experiences in life influence his play? (**AO3**)
- How does Russell relate the events in the play to those in the real world? (**AO3**)

Willy Russell

What is context?

Context is a wide-ranging term. It refers to the historical, socio-economic and political circumstances of the time, as well as to the author's beliefs about those circumstances. It also refers to the way that more personal events in the author's own life may have influenced his thinking and writing. Finally, it may refer to literary context and be concerned with developments in the play as a form that may also have influenced the way it was written.

Russell's early life and education

Willy Russell was born in 1947 into a working-class family near Liverpool. The world he creates in *Blood Brothers* reflects the kind of world he grew up in. His mother worked as a nurse and then in a warehouse. His father had a variety of jobs, mostly working shifts, so was frequently absent from young Willy's life. His father's jobs ranged from working down the mines to managing a fish and chip shop. Russell said of him:

> 'like many people of his generation his life would have been fantastically different if he'd been born into my generation or into a different class, which is what *Blood Brothers* is about.'
>
> (Interview with Jim Mulligan: www.jimmulligan.co.uk/interview/willy-russell-blood-brothers)

It was through his father, who loved political debate, that he first became interested in social inequality.

Russell, an only child, was raised in an environment surrounded by women – while his mother and his grandmother and aunts 'gabbed away' in the kitchen, he would sit under the table, absorbed in their conversations. Although raised in a household that encouraged reading, Russell left school at 15 with only one 'O' Level and became a women's hairdresser. We may speculate that it was this close contact with women that helps him portray female characters (for example, Shirley in *Shirley Valentine*, Rita in *Educating Rita*, and Mrs Johnstone in *Blood Brothers*) in such a sympathetic light. By the age of 20 he felt the need to return to education and, after graduating from university, became a teacher at a comprehensive school in his home city.

During this time Russell wrote songs for performers and for radio shows. In the 1960s the region dominated the pop charts and one of his early plays was about the Liverpool pop group The Beatles. He has a love of popular music and this can be seen in such works as *John, Paul, George, Ringo … and Bert*, *Connie* and, of course, *Blood Brothers*.

Build critical skills

How might Russell's experiences growing up have influenced his writing of *Blood Brothers*? Think not only about his views but also his use of dialogue and his skilful characterisation.

GRADE BOOSTER

Knowing about Russell's background and how it influenced his writing of *Blood Brothers* may help you to write more confidently about the play. You will not be assessed on context on its own, but it is the sign of a high-level candidate to be able to incorporate relevant contextual information into an essay in a constant and informed way.

Social context

Blood Brothers was originally designed as a contemporary school play and had its first performances in Liverpool, where the play itself is set, in 1982. It then transferred to the West End in London for a short run. It was revived three years later, eventually becoming the third longest-running musical in the West End.

The Conservative Party leader, Margaret Thatcher, had been elected prime minister in 1979, three years before the play is set. She claimed that British manufacturing industry had become uncompetitive and saw the cause as being weak employers and overly strong trades unions. The unions were, she felt, too willing to call their members out on strike. She reduced the powers of the workers' unions, privatised ('sold off') many publicly owned companies, and closed many coal mines.

As short-term result, Britain suffered an economic downturn and unemployment soared. This particularly affected industrialised working-class areas in the north of the country, which Willy Russell would have seen first-hand in his home city. Liverpool's famous docks – a traditional source of local employment – were allowed to run down and thousands of households fell into poverty, crime levels increased, housing was allowed to deteriorate and illegal drug use became more common. Some of this context is directly reflected in the play, for example Russell shows the terrible effects of unemployment on Micky's self-esteem. The play explores how poverty and affluence divide society. Thus, we can see that Liverpool is an ideal setting for the events of the play, although, of course, many other towns and cities, especially in northern England, similarly suffered the effects of high unemployment.

▲ Liverpool dock workers

One of Thatcher's central political beliefs was that success comes to those who choose to work hard (see page 43 of this guide). In *Blood Brothers*, Russell contradicts this view. He shows a divided society in which it is the class you are born into that has the greatest influence on your life, regardless of how good or hardworking a person you might be. That money and influential connections are necessary for success is shown by Mickey's failure, despite his good character and hard work. This is the basis of the tragedy of the drama: does 'nature' (the qualities we are born with) or 'nurture' (the environmental factors that influence our upbringing) have the most bearing on the kind of person we become and our success in life? This is known as the 'nature vs nurture' debate (see page 43 of this guide).

Pop culture

In the 1950s, society went through massive social changes. Young people gradually came to have more money and hence popular culture flourished, becoming accessible to a much wider public. Even the poorest in society, people like the Johnstone family, would have had the chance to go to the cinema (nearly every small town and village had at least one cinema) or to a club for dancing.

Various characters in *Blood Brothers* are influenced by music and film. Mrs Johnstone is compared to Marilyn Monroe (see page 50 of this guide) and her love of dancing is an escape from her boring, everyday life. The boys' love of playful but 'violent' games, like 'cowboys and Indians' and 'cops and robbers', is influenced by films.

Literary context

The idea of a Chorus (or Narrator) that comments on the action is an established literary tradition, stretching back to Ancient Greek times. For example, the most powerful effects of one of the most famous Greek tragedies, *Oedipus Rex* (*Oedipus the King*), depends on the audience knowing what will happen. Shakespeare also used this device in some of his plays: for example, the Prologue to *Romeo and Juliet* tells us that 'A pair of star-cross'd lovers take their life'. This knowledge of events can heighten the tension since it shows the audience that there is a lot they still don't know – in *Blood Brothers*, for example, this includes when, why and how the twins will die.

Build critical skills

The Narrator performs the role of a Greek Chorus, narrating, reflecting and interpreting the action on stage. In most productions, he is simply and anonymously dressed in a plain black suit. Why might directors choose to have him appear in this way?

GRADE BOOSTER

To gain high marks in the exam, you need to consider Russell's use of form and structure, such as the use of the Prologue and the Narrator. For example, the fact that Russell reveals the ending of the play at the beginning may suggest that he is less interested in *what* happens than in *why* it happens.

The play needs to be considered as a piece of musical theatre that Russell has constructed, where the music and songs are essential in moving the narrative forward and heightening the atmosphere. Traditionally, musicals used to be simple stories that acted as a vehicle for the songs; the storyline stopped for a song to be sung. Perhaps the first musical to explore a serious theme was *Show Boat* (1927), which tackled the theme of racism. According to Mark Lubbock's *The Complete Book of Light Opera*, *Show Boat* was 'a radical departure in musical storytelling, marrying spectacle with seriousness'. This, however, was unusual for the time. The modern-day musical can be regarded as serious theatre that uses songs to tell the story. The story itself may have a serious message to convey: for example, *Les Misérables* highlights, among other things, the appalling living conditions in nineteenth century France. Another example is *Oh! What A Lovely War*, which is a biting satire on the carnage and folly of World War I, using the musical numbers to great effect in order to reinforce its criticism.

GRADE *FOCUS*

Grade 5

To achieve Grade 5, you will need to show, where appropriate to the exam question, that you have a clear understanding of the context in which the play was written.

Grade 8

To achieve Grade 8, you will need to be able to make perceptive, critical comments about the ways that contextual factors affect the choices the writer makes.

REVIEW YOUR LEARNING

(Answers are given on page 98.)

1. When and where was Willy Russell born?
2. Give examples of the effect of government policy on industry in Liverpool in the 1980s.
3. One of Russell's early plays was about which pop group?
4. Give an example of how popular culture is used by Russell in *Blood Brothers*.
5. What is meant by the 'nature vs nurture' debate?

Plot and structure

Target your thinking

- What are the main events of the play? (**AO1**)
- How do the main storylines develop through the play? (**AO1**, **AO2**)
- How do these events link in to the main themes? (**AO1**, **AO2**)
- How does Russell use dramatic structure? (**AO2**)

The plot of *Blood Brothers* follows the lives of identical twins Mickey and Edward (Eddie), who are separated shortly after birth and brought up in very different surroundings.

The play is divided into two acts. The acts are not divided into scenes, which allows the action to move continuously and inevitably towards its tragic conclusion. To understand the text more clearly and for revision purposes, however, it is easier to break down and summarise the action in smaller sections.

Act One

Section 1

Section 1 is pages 5 to 8 of the Methuen edition.

The play opens virtually at the end! After the overture closes, Mrs Johnstone is heard singing in disbelief 'Tell me it's not true. Say it's just a story' (page 5), followed by the Narrator stepping forward and telling the audience of two boys who were identical twins but were separated. The Narrator asks us to judge their story. The deaths of Mickey and Eddie are then shown, as they will appear in the final moments of the play. The scene fades and Mrs Johnstone takes centre stage, singing her history – of how she fell in love at a dance, got pregnant, married and had seven children before her husband then left her for a younger woman. Her life has been hard – she admits that by the time she was twenty-five she looked like forty-two.

Now Mrs Johnstone can't even afford the basic necessities of life – the milkman (the Narrator in one of his many roles) demands his money and the children complain about always being hungry. On top of this, she is pregnant again. She thinks she will be able to manage, however, when she starts her new job – cleaning a large house for a rich couple called Mr and Mrs Lyons.

Key quotation

Mrs Johnstone: *Tell me it's not true, / Say it's just a story.*
(Page 107)

Build critical skills

Think about the importance of the opening section of *Blood Brothers*. What do you think is the main purpose of this section?

Section 2

Section 2 is pages 8 to 10 of the Methuen edition.

Russell presents Mrs Lyons as a lonely woman despite the fact that she is well off, as her husband works away from home for months at a time and she has no children (but is desperate to conceive). She would like to adopt a child but her husband won't agree to this. The contrast with Mrs Johnstone's situation is clear. Mrs Johnstone's superstitious nature is revealed when Mrs Lyons puts some new shoes on the table – a sign of bad luck. The Narrator enters to reinforce this theme of superstition with more examples of bad luck symbols. Mrs Johnstone finds out that she is expecting twins (the Narrator features again, as the gynaecologist).

Key quotation

Mrs Johnstone: *Oh God, Mrs Lyons, never put new shoes on a table ... You never know what'll happen.*
(Page 9)

GRADE BOOSTER

Commenting on early events that foreshadow later ones shows that you understand Russell's use of structure and how he offers clues to suggest the later fateful unfolding of the tragic events of the play.

Section 3

Section 3 is pages 10 to 16 of the Methuen edition.

Mrs Johnstone is worried that she will not be able to cope with two extra mouths to feed and that Social Services will put more pressure on her to have some of her children put into care. Mrs Lyons sees this as an opportunity to suggest a solution that will help both her and Mrs Johnstone – she will bring one twin up as her own child. Mrs Johnstone is shocked at first but, in awe of the Lyons' wealth and realising that one of her children at least will have a comfortable upbringing, eventually agrees. Mrs Lyons makes Mrs Johnstone swear on the Bible that she will not tell anyone – not even Mr Lyons must know.

Build critical skills

How does Russell suggest the Bible's significance to Mrs Johnstone? What does it suggest about her character?

Section 4

Section 4 is pages 16 to 20 of the Methuen edition.

Mrs Johnstone gives birth to the twins, naming them Mickey and Edward. Various debt collectors arrive, reminding the audience of the financial difficulties Mrs Johnstone is facing. She sings the song 'Easy Terms' (page 17). Mrs Lyons arrives and takes one of the twins. Mrs Johnstone tells the rest of her children that one of the twins has died and gone to heaven.

Section 5

Section 5 is pages 20 to 23 of the Methuen edition.

Mrs Johnstone continues to work at the Lyons' house but now Mrs Lyons is feeling uncomfortable, thinking that Mrs Johnstone is paying too much attention to and getting too attached to the child she gave away. Mrs Lyons fires Mrs Johnstone, giving her money. Mrs Johnstone tries to take the baby and threatens to tell the police but Mrs Lyons terrifies her with a superstition, claiming that both twins will die if they find out about each other. She concludes by saying that if Mrs Johnstone does tell anyone, their deaths will be her fault. Mrs Johnstone leaves without the baby.

Section 6

Section 6 is pages 23 to 37 of the Methuen edition.

Seven years have passed. The Narrator enters and sings a song about superstitions, forewarning the audience that bad things will happen. While he is singing, Mrs Johnstone locks herself in her house – to avoid her many creditors. Mickey, the twin Mrs Johnstone kept, has been playing near the middle-class part of town, much to his mother's concern as she knows the other twin (Edward) lives there. Through song, Mickey tells the audience of his admiration for his elder brother, Sammy. Edward enters and is friendly towards Mickey, giving him some sweets. After establishing that they are the same age and have identical birthdays, they decide to become 'blood brothers'. It is at this point that the term 'blood brothers' is first introduced, which is ironic since they are actual brothers and therefore have no need to become 'blood' brothers. They cut their hands with Mickey's penknife and then clasp their bloody hands together. Mickey explains that they now must always look after each other.

▲ Mickey and Edward become blood brothers

Key quotation

Mickey: *See, this means that we're blood brothers, an' that we always have to stand by each other.*
(Page 30)

Build critical skills

What impression is the audience given of Sammy before we meet him? How is this impression confirmed by his first entrance?

Although equally intelligent, when Mickey whispers the 'F' word Edward says he'll look it up in the dictionary and we learn that Mickey doesn't know what a dictionary is.

Sammy arrives, holding a toy gun, and describes Edward as a posh boy (page 31). Mrs Johnstone enters, realises who Edward is, orders Mickey into the house and sends Edward away (page 33). Later, Mickey calls at the Lyons' house and Mrs Lyons, quickly realising who he is, takes Edward away and tells him not to mix with lower-class boys (page 36). Edward argues and swears at her; she slaps him and immediately regrets her action.

Section 7

Section 7 is pages 37 to 49 of the Methuen edition.

Mickey, Sammy and other children are playing shooting games. The other children laugh at Mickey when he says the '"F" word', saying he will die and go to hell. A girl called Linda appears and defends him. They go to Edward's house and persuade him to sneak out and play with them. Meanwhile, Mrs Lyons is looking for Edward and we get a sense of her over-protective, highly strung nature, as 'in despair' she has called her husband home from work because she is so worried about Edward being missing. Mr Lyons, however, is unsympathetic towards her. Once again the Narrator appears and, adding to the sense of foreboding, reminds us that the devil is close by (page 44).

Influenced by Mickey and Linda, Edward is about to throw stones through some windows when he is caught by a policeman. The policeman first visits Mrs Johnstone and harshly warns her that any more trouble will result in a court appearance. When he visits the Lyons' house, however, he describes the incident as a prank, and advises Mr and Mrs Lyons to make sure he plays with children of his 'own kind', thus underlining the difference that class makes in our society.

Section 8

Section 8 is pages 49 to 58 of the Methuen edition.

Mrs Lyons is worried about the developing friendship between 'her' son and Mickey. She is starting to believe in the superstition she used to frighten Mrs Johnstone (that if the twins meet, they will die) and is becoming afraid of the consequences. She persuades her husband to move to a different house, away in the country. He agrees because he believes (correctly) that she is becoming mentally ill.

When Edward says goodbye to Mickey and Mrs Johnstone, she gives him a locket with a picture of herself and Mickey.

Soon afterwards, Mrs Johnstone hears from the council that she is being re-housed to a less urban area. She is delighted, seeing this as a chance to make a new start, and sings at her good fortune ('Bright New Day'). The neighbours are equally happy that the Johnstone family are moving away!

Key quotation

Mrs Johnstone: *Oh, bright new day / We're goin' away.*
(Page 54)

Act Two

Section 1

Section 1 is pages 59 to 62 of the Methuen edition.

Another seven years have passed and – whether by coincidence or by fate – both families now live in the same area, although no one is aware of this yet.

The act opens with Mrs Johnstone singing about the family's improved fortune – the milkman (Joe) even takes her dancing. Not everything has improved, however – Sammy is on probation for setting the school on fire (he got off lightly because the judge was attracted to Mrs Johnstone). Every day she thinks about the twin she gave away. Mickey is an awkward teenager at the local mixed comprehensive school and is becoming aware of girls. In contrast, Edward is at an all-boys private boarding school.

Section 2

Section 2 is pages 62 to 70 of the Methuen edition.

Mickey is on the school bus with Linda when Sammy joins them. Sammy is on 'the dole' (i.e. unemployed and on state benefits) and he tries to get a cheap schoolchild's ticket but the conductor refuses. Sammy threatens him with a knife and tries to steal the conductor's money bag before running off, chased by a policeman. Linda tells Mickey that she loves him – but that he had better not turn out a criminal like his brother.

Edward gets into trouble at school and is suspended for refusing to give the teacher the locket Mrs Johnstone gave him; at the same time, Mickey (and Linda) is also being suspended, for insolence to the teacher.

Mrs Lyons is angered by Edward's suspension and by seeing the locket, as she realises she hasn't completely broken the link with Mrs Johnstone and Mickey.

The Narrator sings another warning about the devil being close to you and knowing where you are. This adds to the tension that is slowly building up.

Build critical skills

How does Russell suggest the similarities between Sammy, Mickey and Edward in this section and what effect does this create?

Section 3

Section 3 is pages 70 to 77 of the Methuen edition.

Mickey and Linda go for a walk up a high hill, where they see a 'lad' looking out of his window. Linda thinks he is 'gorgeous' but Mickey doesn't like her saying that, although he can't admit to her how he feels about her. Linda leaves in a huff.

GRADE BOOSTER

Simply recounting the plot will not gain you a high grade. Examination questions require you to write about how a theme or character is presented by the writer. Always think in terms of *how* not *what*.

The boy who was looking out of his window approaches – it is Edward. The audience hears them both wish that they looked more like the other ('That Guy'). Once they recognise each other Mickey confides to Edward that he doesn't know how to tell Linda he loves her. Edward suggests they go to see sex films at the cinema to learn about sex. They return to Mickey's house for some money; Russell shows that Mrs Johnstone is delighted to see Edward again and joins in their humour about the film they are going to see.

Once again the Narrator adds a sense of foreboding – it is said that the devil has been seen standing close to you.

Section 4

Section 4 is pages 77 to 79 of the Methuen edition.

Mrs Lyons turns up at Mrs Johnstone's house, wanting to know if Mrs Johnstone is going to follow her forever. She attempts to bribe Mrs Johnstone with money to move away from the area but Mrs Johnstone refuses as she has made a better life for herself here in her new home. Mrs Lyons grabs a kitchen knife and lunges at Mrs Johnstone, who is able to avoid the attempted stabbing. Mrs Lyons leaves, cursing Mrs Johnstone as a 'witch' (page 79). Off-stage, children's voices are heard chanting a song about the woman who is mad, in reference to Mrs Lyons, who is now clearly in the process of a mental breakdown.

Key quotation

Mrs Lyons: *I curse the day I met you. You ruined me.*
(Page 79)

Section 5

Section 5 is pages 79 to 81 of the Methuen edition.

We see Edward and Mickey leave the cinema, thrilled by what they have seen and easily falling back into their old friendship, together with Linda. This is exemplified by an incident with a policeman, echoing the earlier incident of the stone-throwing.

Key quotation

Edward: *we have been undergoing a remarkable celluloid experience!*

Mickey: *We've been to the pictures.*
(Page 80)

Section 6

Section 6 is pages 82 to 87 of the Methuen edition.

We fast-forward four years through a series of short tableaux (fairground, chip shop, beach) that show Edward, Mickey and Linda becoming close friends.

Their time together comes to an end when they are eighteen years old, when Edward tells Linda he is leaving for university the next day. We learn that Mickey is already working in a factory. Edward is shocked to learn that Mickey still hasn't told Linda how he feels about her. He asks her if he can write her letters. He sings lovingly ('I'm Not Saying A Word') that, if he were Mickey, he would have asked her out a long time ago but out of loyalty to his friend he can only hint at his true feelings for her. When

Mickey arrives Edward urges him to declare his feelings for Linda. Eventually Mickey asks her out and they kiss, becoming boyfriend and girlfriend. They invite Edward to come to a club with them but Edward, dejected, declines.

Section 7

Section 7 is pages 87 to 90 of the Methuen edition.

The action moves to October and the scene opens on Mrs Johnstone's house, where Mickey is telling his mother that Linda is pregnant and that they are getting married in a month's time. On their wedding day, Mickey is sacked from his job ('Miss Jones'). Mr Lyons, the managing director, blames the 'global slump' and says it is a sign of the economic recession (page 88). Mr Lyons represents the uncaring attitude of management – he even gets his secretary, Miss Jones, to type out her own redundancy notice (pages 89–90)!

Section 8

Section 8 is pages 90 to 95 of the Methuen edition.

That Christmas, Edward comes home from university happy and contented with life, in sharp contrast to Mickey who is dejected. While Edward has been partying and making new friends, Mickey has been out of work for the last three months. Edward cannot understand the problems of living life 'on the dole'. Mickey explains that while he has had to grow up, Edward can still happily play around like a kid. He feels that they no longer have anything in common and reacts angrily when Edward offers him money, telling him to go away before he hits him.

As he leaves, Edward bumps into Linda, while Mickey meets Sammy. As Edward's friendship with Mickey is now ended, Edward can declare his true feelings for Linda, and asks her to marry him. She informs him that she has married Mickey and is expecting his baby.

While this conversation is going on, Sammy is persuading Mickey to act as look-out for a robbery at a petrol station, offering him £50.

Build critical skills

How does Russell bring out the contrasting attitudes of Mickey and Edward in this section? Which of the boys do you most sympathise with and why?

Section 9

Section 9 is pages 95 to 96 of the Methuen edition.

The Narrator enters and warns that everything has its price. The robbery goes wrong and Sammy kills the filling-station attendant. He and Mickey run to their house and hide the gun, but both are arrested.

Section 10

Section 10 is pages 96 to 100 of the Methuen edition.

Mrs Johnstone informs the audience that Mickey was sent to prison for seven years for his part in the robbery. While in prison he became clinically depressed and dependent on antidepressants. Released from prison early, he is a shadow of his former self, 'feelin' fifteen years older' (page 98), and is now addicted to the tablets.

Linda has found Mickey a job but refuses to tell Mrs Johnstone how she managed it. Linda and Mickey have moved into their own home, but Mickey is still addicted to his antidepressants. Linda desperately tries to convince him that they have sorted out their lives and he does not need the pills. Mickey is angry and answers that he knows who really sorted their lives out: having helped them earlier with sweets and cigarettes, Edward, now Councillor Lyons, has gone on to give them a job and their house. Mickey demands the drugs and doesn't care about his life anymore, wanting to be 'invisible' to the world. Even when Linda says she doesn't love him when he takes drugs, he still demands them.

Section 11

Section 11 is pages 100 to 104 of the Methuen edition.

The scene changes to Linda arranging to meet Edward while the Narrator and Mrs Johnstone comment on their 'light romance'. It is unclear to the audience whether Linda and Edward are having only a light romance or an actual affair. Meanwhile, Mickey is at work and trying desperately not to take his drugs. Mrs Lyons enters and tells Mickey that Edward and Linda are seeing each other. In a frenzied state Mickey rushes home and takes Sammy's gun, which was hidden under the floorboards. He frantically searches the town while the Narrator comments that a killing is about to happen. Mrs Johnstone finds Linda; Linda realises that Mickey is after Edward, who is attending a meeting at the Town Hall.

Section 12

Section 12 is pages 104 to 106 of the Methuen edition.

A confident, self-assured Edward is chairing a meeting. There is a commotion when Mickey enters, pointing his gun at Edward, and the rest of the councillors rush off. Mickey accuses Edward of betrayal and blames him for taking Linda away from him, ironically commenting that although they were blood brothers he has got nothing out of life while Edward has been given everything. He even accuses Edward of fathering Linda's child, Sarah; we know this is not true but it is a sign of Mickey's depression and desperate state of mind.

Key quotation

Mickey: *Well, how come you got everything … an' I got nothin'?* (Page 105)

Section 13

Section 13 is pages 106 to 107 of the Methuen edition.

The police and Mrs Johnstone arrive and in an attempt to stop Mickey shooting Edward, Mrs Johnstone decides to reveal the truth to Mickey: that Edward is his twin brother who was given away at birth to Mrs Lyons (ironically, Mickey had just told Edward that he 'can't even' shoot him, page 106). The revelation has the opposite of the intended effect. Instead of calming Mickey, it makes him worse and he screams in anger at his mother, asking why she couldn't have given him away so that he would have been the one to have had the better life. In his anger he waves the gun at Edward. It accidently goes off, killing Edward. The police then shoot Mickey. He dies.

Key quotation

Mickey: *I could have been ... I could have been him!'*
(Page 106)

Section 14

Section 14 is pages 107 to 108 of the Methuen edition.

The play ends with Mrs Johnstone lamenting what has happened. The Narrator highlights the key theme of the play by asking the question of the audience:

> And do we blame superstition for what came to pass?
> Or could it be what we, the English, have come to know as class?
> (Page 107)

Structure

Perhaps the first noticeable aspect of the structure of the play is Russell showing us the ending at the beginning. The idea of knowing what's going to happen from the start may appear a little strange to modern-day audiences (and readers and TV viewers) who are used to thrillers and crime stories but, as we have seen (page 13), it is following a tradition dating at least back to Ancient Greece.

Another noticeable feature of the play is the use of a Narrator who speaks to the audience at the beginning and throughout the play, commenting on the action and setting the scene. He gradually gets more aggressive with each song he sings, constantly reminding the audience of the brothers' fate. See pages 37–39 of this guide for a detailed analysis of his role.

As noted above, *Blood Brothers* is divided into two acts. The first act sets the scene, provides relevant background information and introduces the main characters. The chain of events that will eventually lead to the tragic deaths of the twins is set in motion, although the act ends on a high note with Mrs Johnstone celebrating the news that the family are moving to a new house in the country. The second act starts off on the same high note but an undercurrent of foreboding is never far away: the boys get suspended and Mrs Lyons tries to stab Mrs Johnstone. The happy teenage years are contrasted with the devastating effects of unemployment that lead to the tragic denouement and the price that has to be paid. Thus the play has come full circle: the stage directions tell us that the opening scene shows us the very end of the play where Mickey and Edward die.

GRADE BOOSTER

Understanding the structure of *Blood Brothers* may help you to write more confidently about some of the ideas in the play. You will not be assessed on structure alone, but it is the sign of a high-level candidate to be able to incorporate relevant analysis of the play's structure in an informed way. You need to be able to comment on how Russell has structured the play to emphasise such themes as the inevitability of the twins' fate (see pages 45-47 of this guide).

The play is presented through a series of short episodes without a break, which allows the action to move swiftly and smoothly from one event to the next. This provides Russell with an opportunity to contrast the lifestyle of a working-class family (the Johnstones) with that of a middle-class family (the Lyons). A scene involving Mrs Johnstone and Mickey is often shortly followed by a scene involving the Lyons family. After the audience has learned about Mickey's life of poverty and hardship (for example, his mother locking the door in case the rent man comes; Sammy breaking his toys) we are presented with a stereotypical picture of middle-class contentment: Edward and his father play-fighting on the floor, then his mother reading him a storybook with Mr Lyons sitting with them on the arm of the chair. An even clearer of example of Russell's use of juxtaposition of scenes is shown by the police reaction to the boys' crime: Edward's mother gets advice from the policeman to be sure her son plays with boys from his own social class (page 48). In contrast, Mickey is automatically viewed with suspicion and Mrs Johnstone is told by the police that any further events Mickey is involved in will mean appearing in court 'or worse'.

Timeframe

It is impossible to be exact about the timeframe of *Blood Brothers* but it seems to take place over a period of no longer than about twenty-five years. At the start, Mrs Johnstone is pregnant with the twins. They are born and Mrs Lyons takes one and sacks Mrs Johnstone. The scene then jumps forward seven years to when we first meet Mickey and Edward. After that another seven years passes, anc then through a series of short tableaux Mickey, Edward and Linda reach eighteen years when Edward starts university. Mickey is given seven years in prison but gets out early and gets a job. Edward has finished university and become a councillor by the time of his and Mickey's deaths.

GRADE *FOCUS*

Grade 5

To achieve a Grade 5, you will show a clear and detailed understanding of the whole text and of the effects created by its structure.

Grade 8

To achieve a Grade 8, your response will display a comprehensive understanding of explicit and implicit meanings in the text as a whole and will examine and evaluate the writer's use of structure in detail.

REVIEW YOUR LEARNING

(Answers are given on page 98.)

1. Give one advantage of the play not being divided into separate scenes.
2. How much older than her actual years does Mrs Johnstone look?
3. How does Mrs Johnstone meet Mrs Lyons?
4. What is the first indication of Mrs Johnstone's superstitious nature?
5. How does Mrs Johnstone explain to the rest of her children that she now has only one of the twins?
6. List three of the 'shooting games' the children play in Act One.
7. What does Sammy do when the bus conductor refuses to sell him the cheap schoolchildren's fare?
8. List three of the places Mickey, Edward and Linda go to as teenagers.
9. Give one function of the Narrator.
10. What two possibilities does the Narrator suggest could be responsible for what has happened in the play?

Characterisation

Target your thinking

- Who are the key characters? (**AO1**)
- What role does each character play? (**AO1**, **AO2**)
- How does Russell present the characters to us? (**AO2**)

There are relatively few characters in *Blood Brothers* and they are all defined by their social class. Their attitudes are largely fixed – although Mickey and Edward do grow and change as the play develops, their development is still defined by their social class. The friendship they develop across the social divide is doomed by external forces.

GRADE BOOSTER

Always remember that a play is written to be performed in front of an audience, not just to be read in class! It's what an audience *sees* and *hears* that determines its attitude to any particular character, and to the play as a whole. Bear this in mind when answering a question on *Blood Brothers*.

Russell presents the characters in *Blood Brothers* through a combination of techniques:

- What the characters say.
- What the characters do.
- What other characters say to them and about them.
- Through stage directions, lighting, props, costume, music and other aspects of stagecraft.

Mrs Johnstone

Key quotation

Mrs Johnstone: *By the time I was twenty-five, / I looked like forty-two*
(Page 6)

Russell presents Mrs Johnstone as a woman in her mid-twenties at the start of the play, who has already had seven children. Russell creates sympathy for her by telling us how these births have sapped her strength and taken away her beauty. Due to the social conventions of the time, whereby to be an unmarried mother was a disgrace to herself and her whole family, Mrs Johnstone had to get married when she first became pregnant. Eventually, however, her husband left her for a younger woman, leaving her poor and expecting twins (read again her opening song: 'Marilyn Monroe', pages 5–6).

She is presented as a maternal, caring character and a kind and loving mother. Her personal circumstances, however, make it difficult to describe her as a 'good' mother. Russell shows how she has problems disciplining her children and keeping them under control: when Sammy burns the school down she blames the school for letting Sammy play with dangerous chemicals (page 59). Her lack of control over her children can lead to humorous situations, such as when they first arrive at their new home and Sammy tries to ride a cow (off-stage) which in fact is a bull, while Donna Marie steps into something rather nasty (page 57). But of course you may also consider that Russell presents her lack of parental control as a contributory factor in Sammy's criminal behaviour that will eventually lead to the death of her twins.

▲ Mrs Johnstone, played by Stephanie Lawrence

Mrs Johnstone's poverty forces her to buy things on the 'never never' (also known as hire purchase). This method of purchase means that you don't own the goods until the last payment has been made; if you miss a payment the goods are taken away from you. Russell shows that this is what invariably happens to the Johnstone family.

GRADE BOOSTER

To gain the highest levels you should be able to explore how Russell links the idea of living on the 'never never' with the price to be paid for giving away one of the twins. The Narrator constantly reminds us of this: 'But a debt is a debt, and must be paid' (page 16), and Mrs Johnstone herself recognises the irony of the situation in her song 'Easy Terms' (page 17).

Russell shows Mrs Johnstone often making rash, impulsive decisions without thinking about the consequences of her actions. This is clearly seen when she buys goods she can't afford and they get repossessed. More importantly, Russell uses this personality trait he has created in Mrs Johnstone to show how she can give up one of the twins so easily.

Mrs Johnstone has a strong and generous nature, however – bringing up seven children single-handedly shows her strength of character. She

Build critical skills

The Narrator describes Mrs Johnstone at the beginning of the play as having 'a stone in place of her heart'. Challenging this view, with textual support, is a sign that you are thinking carefully about the text and coming to your own conclusions. Who really is the mother with a heart of stone?

refuses Mrs Lyons' attempt to 'buy her off' and throws the money away, shocked at the suggestion. Here, Russell reveals her strong maternal instinct and that she values people above money, even though she is so poor.

When she does agree to give up her child, her motives are clearly presented as unselfish: she stares mesmerised at the grandeur of Mrs Lyons' house and considers how much better her child's life would be if he was brought up by the Lyons.

She also has sympathy for Mr and Mrs Lyons' inability to have children, recognising the irony of Mrs Lyons living childless in a large house, while she can get pregnant so easily.

It is under extreme pressure, then, that Mrs Johnstone agrees to give up her child, foreseeing a much better future for him. Therefore, it can be argued that she is misguided rather than hard-hearted. She does find it difficult, and when she is sacked as Mrs Lyons' cleaner and unable to see her child every day, she attempts to take him back. She is thwarted by Mrs Lyons using Mrs Johnstone's naivety and her superstitious nature against her, telling her of the 'curse' of twins separated at birth discovering each other's existence, which she knows will terrify Mrs Johnstone.

Mrs Johnstone places little value on education, being uneducated herself. Perhaps this is linked to her highly superstitious nature. She appears unconcerned when Mickey and Sammy are suspended from school.

Perhaps linked to her superstitious nature is her fatalistic attitude to life: what will be, will be. She never concerns herself with trying to explain or understand what happens in her life; she simply accepts that whatever happens is her 'fate'. This attitude could explain her happy-go-lucky and down-to-earth outlook, which gives her a zest for life. Russell demonstrates this in her love of dancing and in how, when Mickey asks for money to see a soft porn movie with Edward, she joins in the humour.

Build critical skills

Do you think Mrs Lyons would have reacted in the same way as Mrs Johnstone to finding out that her son intended to watch a pornographic film (page 76)? How do such reactions help shape the audience's attitude towards these two characters?

The move to the country is presented as a dream come true, although the family can't completely change their habits as Sammy burns down the school. True to her nature, however, Mrs Johnstone defends him, blaming the school for allowing him to play with dangerous chemicals.

Key quotation

Mrs Johnstone: *I know I shouldn't, you soft get. I've spent all me bleedin' life knowin'* I shouldn't. *But I do. Now take y' soddin' wireless an' get off.*
(Page 17)

Key quotation

Mrs Johnstone: *Me husband used to say that all we had to do was shake hands and I'd be in the club.*
(Pages 8–9)

Build critical skills

Consider whether Mrs Lyons believes the superstition she tells Mrs Johnstone or if she is making it up, knowing Mrs Johnstone's superstitious nature. If the latter, what does this tell us about Mrs Lyons?

When she gives Edward the locket containing a picture of her and Mickey, it is supposedly intended to remind Edward of his friendship with Mickey, but it also shows that she can't quite give up her link with Edward.

When Mickey tells her that Linda is pregnant, she is understanding and compassionate, recognising that she was in exactly the same position. She is non-judgemental of people. Also, for perhaps the first time in the play, she goes into a reflective mood where she considers the type of life Mickey has had with her. Mickey quickly dismisses her concerns, revealing the close bond between the two.

She is helpless, however, as Mickey's life disintegrates and can only watch in despair. She does try to intervene at the Council meeting but is rejected by Mickey. Her final song reveals her heartbreak and sorrow.

Mrs Lyons

While having some characteristics in common, such as the value they place on motherhood and being of a similar age, in many ways Mrs Lyons is presented by Russell as the exact opposite of Mrs Johnstone in terms of material possessions, social class and personality. Mrs Lyons and her husband are wealthy and own a large house, while Mrs Johnstone is stuck in poverty and rents a council house.

Russell presents Mrs Lyons as a middle-class, childless housewife who is possibly lonely and unfulfilled as she is often alone in a large, child-free house. Her husband initially works abroad (thus enabling her to 'have' the baby) and later has his own business. Although pampered with a very comfortable lifestyle, she is an inconsiderate and self-centred individual who at times bullies and uses others for her own gain. This is clearly seen when she manipulates Mrs Johnstone's vulnerability, gullibility and superstitious nature to get one of the twins. She goes to great lengths to keep up the pretence of pregnancy and, once she has the baby, sacks Mrs Johnstone and uses emotional and financial blackmail to keep her away from Edward.

Key quotation

Mrs Lyons: *You won't tell anyone about this, Mrs Johnstone, because if you do, you will kill them.*
(Page 23)

We see Russell presenting Mrs Lyons as a snobbish and over-protective mother as Edward grows up, 'smothering' him with love. She is continually anxious about him; we can speculate that this anxiety may be caused by her knowledge that Edward is not truly her son. She is living a lie and lives in fear of discovery; this fear eventually drives her mad.

By the time of her mental breakdown, Russell shows that she may have actually come to believe in the superstition about twins separated at birth. This contradicts her early comment to Mrs Johnstone that an adopted child can become like 'one's own' (page 8), which comes before the idea of taking one of the twins is thought of.

This is a good example of Russell's use of irony, as it foreshadows Mrs Lyons' later breakdown. Her breakdown makes it clear that no matter how much she tries, she cannot cope with the fact that Edward is not really her son. She seems to have felt guilt at an early stage about taking Edward away from Mrs Johnstone, as even when he was a tiny baby she would think that Edward knew that he was not her real son. This guilt appears to have gnawed away at her over the years, gradually unhinging her mind. Mr Lyons recognises his wife's depression, suggesting that she see a doctor and get something for her 'nerves'. Edward also later worries about her mental state and when she fails to recognise Mickey in the locket, thinking it is Edward, he asks her if she has become ill again.

Build critical skills

Why do you think Russell includes the scene with the locket, where Mrs Lyons thinks it is Edward who has been photographed with Mrs Johnstone, instead of Mickey? Could this be a symbol of her guilt or that she is not the real mother? Try offering in your responses more than one view or explanation of why an event or dialogue is included.

She becomes more paranoid when she finds out that the Johnstone family have also moved to the country. She accuses Mrs Johnstone of following her and fears that she will never be able to escape. Her mental breakdown becomes complete when, in one of the most dramatic moments in the play, she attempts to kill Mrs Johnstone with a kitchen knife. The Narrator (as Kids) comments that Mrs Lyons has become insane.

Her final words in the play are to curse Mrs Johnstone as a witch for ruining her life (page 79). She has one more significant action to perform, however, in that she sets in motion the final chain of events that leads to the deaths of the twins: she informs Mickey of Edward and Linda's relationship. The moment she points out Linda and Edward to Mickey (page 103) is, dramatically, one of the most tension-filled moments in the play. The audience can sense that this could be the beginning of the end. The fact that it is done silently, and not through dialogue as we might have expected, adds to the tension. Mrs Lyons is presented at this moment as a shadowy, ghostly figure, much like the terrifying Ghost of Christmas Yet to Come in Dickens' *Christmas Carol* – a faceless, silent phantom representing our worst fears of the future. Only here there is no chance of a reprieve: the twins are doomed.

Build critical skills

Look back over the scenes where Mrs Lyons appears, to locate any moments when Russell encourages sympathy for her from the audience. This will help you gather evidence to show her desperation and any misguided actions that give her character more depth and complexity.

Mickey

Russell presents Mickey at the beginning of the play as a friendly, curious boy aged seven (nearly eight!) being brought up in a poor area of Liverpool. Significantly, in view of later events, he first appears with a toy gun. He plays games on the streets with his brothers, sisters and other local children that are inspired by TV and cinema. Living in a large family, Russell presents him as looking up to his elder brother, Sammy, and being in awe of the things Sammy can do, like weeing through people's letter-boxes. Sammy does, however, bully Mickey at times, for example taking his toy car and breaking it. Russell shows Mickey, perhaps worryingly, wanting to emulate his wilder elder brother and finding it hard to say no to Sammy.

Russell presents this idolising of Sammy partially in order to explain why Mickey agrees to join Sammy in robbing the service station. Russell presents Mickey's first words in the play as revealing his working-class, Liverpudlian background (see page 24).

Throughout the play Russell distinguishes the social division between Mickey and Edward by Mickey speaking in a Liverpool dialect, in contrast to the Standard English used by his twin, Edward. Although Russell's use of dialect in the play is affectionate, he is perhaps suggesting that Standard English has a higher status and therefore that its use by Edward may open doors in society that remain closed to Mickey.

Mickey has a very open, friendly personality, like his mother, and seems to have a special bond with her, perhaps due to Mrs Johnstone's guilt at giving away his twin. When Edward appears, Russell shows them very quickly becoming firm friends (not surprising, since they are identical twins) and 'blood brothers'.

In the 'kids games' Russell shows how Mickey is protected by Linda, who clearly has a crush on him. Mickey accepts Linda as an equal, even though he thinks that girls aren't as good as boys (page 42), and they become lifelong friends, eventually marrying. Mickey and Linda are presented as enjoying childish pranks, impressing Edward with their bravado and anti-authoritarian attitude – until they meet a real policeman!

Key quotation

Mickey: *Do you wanna be my blood brother, Eddie?*
(Page 30)

Build critical skills

Why do you think Russell chooses to include these childhood games and pranks? In what way do they prepare the audience for events later in the play?

When Edward moves away, Mickey is lost without him. Russell shows him expressing these feelings, which are mirrored by Edward, in his song 'Long Sunday Afternoon' (page 53).

As he enters adolescence, Russell shows Mickey's shyness and awkwardness with girls, especially Linda. He initially regards Linda as only a friend, while she constantly claims to be in love with him, which he finds embarrassing. Mickey continues to find it very hard to express his feelings about Linda and it takes years, and a push from Edward, to ask her out on a date.

Russell uses the twins' experiences at school both to highlight their differences in social class and also to remind the audience that, being twins, Mickey and Edward share some of the same personality traits. Mickey gets suspended for ridiculing the teacher and being defiant; Edward is also suspended for showing similar defiance.

GRADE BOOSTER

Examination questions may ask you to consider how a particular character is used to present a theme. For example, 'How does Russell present the theme of social class through Mickey and Edward?' Learn to think of characters in this way.

Build critical skills

Why do you think Russell excludes Edward from the wedding? In what way does this prepare us for later events in the play? How does Edward's ignorance about Mickey and Linda's marriage add to the drama?

Russell presents Mickey's late teens with Edward and Linda as the happiest time of his life. Russell shows this through a series of brief tableaux showing the three of them at the fairground, chip shop and beach. In many ways Mickey and Edward complement each other and each wishes he were like the other: Mickey likes Edward's generosity and is able to show Edward a different kind of life to that which he is used to. Edward also gives Mickey a chance to escape the oppression he feels from poverty, school and even his brother Sammy.

We begin to see a difference emerging between Mickey and Edward because of their education and upbringing; while both are inexperienced with girls, Mickey is unable to find the words when he wants to ask Linda out. On the other hand Edward is able to be quite poetic in what he would say to Linda. This difference becomes more pronounced after Edward goes to university while Mickey is stuck in a dead-end job.

Mickey works hard to provide for his family and he works overtime even though he hates his job. He then marries Linda rather quickly as she is pregnant, but immediately loses his job.

Russell shows how the difference in Edward's and Mickey's social class and educational opportunity lead to them falling out; they have nothing in common now and do not understand each other's worlds. Mickey has had to grow up too quickly and learn about the reality of life on the 'dole', while Edward has led a sheltered life both at a private school and then at university.

Build critical skills

Read the dialogue between Mickey and Edward when Edward comes back home from university (pages 91–93). What does this dialogue between Mickey and Edward tell us about their respective attitudes and experiences of life? How does Russell suggest Mickey's attitude to Edward in this dialogue?

It is Mickey's desperation to escape a life of poverty and provide for Linda and their baby that leads to him accepting Sammy's offer of £50 to act as a look-out in the hold-up. Russell is perhaps highlighting a strong link between poverty and crime. Prison is not presented as in any way positive or helpful. It has a devastating effect on Mickey, who becomes clinically depressed and dependent on antidepressants. When he is released from prison, Russell shows Mickey as having aged greatly. He is now a changed man.

Key quotation

Mrs Johnstone: *You'd think he was dead / Like Marilyn Monroe*
(Page 98)

GRADE BOOSTER

Recognising how Russell uses the Marilyn Monroe motif (see pages 50-52 of this guide) to refer to Mickey now, instead of Mrs Johnstone, shows an appreciation of the writer's skills. Notice, however, that this time the motif is used to highlight negative aspects of Monroe's life, reflecting Mickey's decline and foreshadowing his death.

Mickey's dependency on his tablets places a great strain on his marriage. He now feels useless and a total failure as he knows it was Councillor Eddie Lyons who provided the job and house – providing these should be a husband's role in Mickey's eyes.

Russell shows that when Mickey finds out about Edward and Linda his jealousy and hurt pride blind him to reason and he goes in search of Edward with the gun used by Sammy for the hold-up. He even accuses Edward of being responsible for Linda's pregnancy.

Build critical skills

Look at the section on page 105 where Mickey and Edward are alone on the Council platform.

(Page 105)

What does Russell's sentence structure in this dialogue suggest about Mickey's state of mind at this moment?

GRADE BOOSTER

If you can understand the answer to that question ('How come you got everything ... an' I got nothin'?'), you are well on the way to appreciating Russell's key message of *Blood Brothers*.

Russell does make it clear, however, that Edward's death is accidental when Mickey tells Edward that he thought he was going to shoot him but that he now can't.

At the end he breaks his mother's heart when he asks her why he wasn't the one she gave away, and reveals all the anguish and sufferings of his life when he screams, 'I could have been ... I could have been him' (page 106). Russell very simply states the theme that dominates the whole play when Mickey asks Edward:

> How come you got everything ... an' I got nothin'?
>
> (Page 105)

Edward

Key quotation

Edward: *Pissed off. You say smashing things don't you?*
(Page 28)

Russell presents Edward as an only child in a middle-class home with an over-protective mother and a father who is often away, working. The audience first see him when he meets Mickey. His first word, 'Hello', reveals a polite boy who speaks in Standard English with a 'posh' accent, in contrast to Mickey's working-class language and accent. In his first conversation with Mickey Russell presents Edward as a generous, friendly seven-year-old who gladly shares his sweets. He has led a sheltered life and is fascinated by Mickey's knowledge of rude words. He is not normally allowed to play on the street and does not appear to have any friends apart from Mickey.

Even at this early age, Russell contrasts their differing views on education: Edward intends to look up the meaning of a word in a dictionary, while Mickey doesn't even know what a dictionary is. Like Mickey, Edward has a toy gun – given to him by his father. Even in this presentation of the 'ideal' middle-class family at home, then, Russell seems to add an undercurrent of violence, foreshadowing future events.

Edward is impressed with Linda and Mickey's pranks and when he moves away he is lost without Mickey. He mirrors Mickey's loneliness as expressed in the song on page 53. As we have seen, Russell also uses a mirroring technique when Mickey's suspension from school is mirrored by Edward's. This reinforces the identical genetic make-up of the twins, who therefore share the same personality traits. We have already had a hint of Edward's rebellious nature when he calls his mother a 'fuckoff' (page 36) and is cheeky to the policeman (page 81).

As he enters adolescence, Russell shows us that Edward, like Mickey, is awkward with girls. For Edward, part of this awkwardness could be because he goes to an all-boys public school and hardly ever sees a girl. His education and reading, however, mean he is more articulate and can tell Mickey what to say to them – although, like Mickey, he has had no practical experience of meeting girls. Russell uses humour to present the boys' naivety and inexperience when they decide to go to the cinema to watch a soft porn film in order to learn about sex (page 74). Mrs Johnstone joins in the fun with her down-to-earth attitude. This greatly impresses Edward who regards her as 'fabulous', although Mickey is more shocked by his mother's attitude.

Mickey, Edward and Linda are at their happiest during their teenage years before Edward goes to university. Russell, however, reveals the first signs of potential conflicting loyalties emerging when Edward hints at his feelings for Linda by asking if he can write to her when he's at university. Out of loyalty to Mickey, he won't explicitly express his feelings to Linda, although Russell makes sure that the audience (and Linda herself) are left in no doubt about the way he feels towards her with his song on page 85.

It may be that being at university and backed financially by his parents means that Edward is leading a sheltered life and is unable to understand Mickey's life of poverty. On page 92, although trying to help, he unwittingly insults Mickey, angering him by trying to give him money.

GRADE BOOSTER

Notice how, in this song, Russell emphasises the greater confidence and educational achievement of Edward compared to Mickey, through Edward's use of irony and Shakespearian **allusion**.

Allusion: an indirect reference to well-known literature or music that the writer assumes the audience will recognise. In this case, when Edward sings 'How can I compare thee to a summer's day' he is referring to Shakespeare's famous Sonnet 18.

Build critical skills

Do you think Edward lacks compassion and sympathy for Mickey's plight when he asks him if a job is important and why he doesn't just live off the dole? Or does he want to help, but doesn't know how and can't understand Mickey's situation as he has never had to face poverty himself?

When he finally declares his love for Linda it is too late; she is married and expecting Mickey's baby. Russell presents Edward now as a respected member of his community, he is a councillor on the Housing Committee and so is able to help Mickey, Linda and their daughter get a house of their own instead of living with Mrs Johnstone. He is also able to get Mickey a job in his father's factory. The secrecy surrounding this help, however, makes the situation between Edward and Mickey worse once Mickey finds out. Edward claims that he and Linda are just friends but Mickey refuses to believe this, and Edward dies after Mickey's gun accidently goes off. Russell thus shows the audience that the superstitious prediction with which Mrs Lyons threatened Mrs Johnstone at the beginning of the play has come true.

Linda

Russell presents Linda as being of the same age and social class as Mickey. She protects and mothers him when he is mocked by the other children during their games (page 41), thus establishing her kind and compassionate nature. She also comes to his aid when he gets suspended from school (resulting in her own suspension) and constantly lets everybody know she loves him – much to Mickey's embarrassment.

She is, however, more than just a stereotypically feminine nurturing character. Russell presents her as having unrealised potential. As a child she appears as a feisty, quick-witted girl who often leads the way in the games with Mickey and Edward. She can out-shoot both of them and she plays a trick on the policeman so the three of them can escape.

As we have seen, the teenage years are happy times for Linda, Edward and Mickey, but even here Russell casts a shadow over their future. When Linda misses her shots in the rifle range (page 82) Russell may be hinting that all may not be well in her future. The Narrator reinforces this sense of foreboding in a more explicit way when he talks about the fate of young lambs and the pain Linda will face in the future.

GRADE BOOSTER

What other examples of irony can you find in the play? Make a list of them to have at your fingertips in the examination.

Like for her mother-in-law, Mrs Johnstone, social conventions demand that Linda gets married once she becomes pregnant. Once married to Mickey, Russell shows her as being very supportive but fearful for him whenever Sammy is around, as she is well aware of the bad influence he is on her husband. While admitting to Edward that she has always loved him in some way (page 94), she intends to be faithful to Mickey. In desperation, however, she secretly goes to Edward for help. Her evasive answers to Mrs Johnstone's questions reveal her guilt in asking Edward for help. The irony of her reply as to the identity of this benefactor (page 99) should not be lost on the audience.

The daily grind of living a life in poverty begins to take its toll. Russell uses a visual image to convey this: the stage directions suggest that Linda is beginning to look old and tired before her time (page 98). The audience can see how she is becoming like her mother-in-law, who looked forty-two when she was twenty-five (page 6). Russell seems to be presenting a vicious circle for working-class women, seeing them as trapped by their poverty and becoming old before their time.

Linda is presented as strong-willed and she tries to help Mickey become less dependent on his tablets, but seemingly without success.

A key issue in the play is Linda's relationship with Edward: do they actually have an affair or, as Edward claims, are they just friends? We know that Linda loves Edward and may have fallen out of love with Mickey once he became a drug addict, but she is supportive of him and approaches Edward for help for her family. Edward too is presented as loving Linda, but he has always been loyal to Mickey in the past and does say to Mickey that he and Linda are just friends. Mrs Johnstone, perhaps the most reliable source of evidence, states that it is just 'a light romance' and that there is nothing sinister or immoral in their relationship (page 102).

Mrs Johnstone also sings, however, that they shouldn't have become so friendly, knowing their feelings for each other (pages 101–02). As Linda is talking to Edward, the Narrator comments that Linda is remembering the freedom of her youthful days and is wondering what price she will have to pay if she gives way to her childhood feelings (page 101).

Russell's stage directions are also significant at this point as they do kiss and hold hands (page 102). Is this enough evidence of an affair? Mrs Lyons certainly thinks so, as she draws Mickey's attention to Linda and Edward together (page 103).

Build critical skills

Do you think Linda and Edward have an affair or, despite their feelings for each other, just remain friends? Does it affect your attitude to Linda, Edward or Mickey? What do you think is Russell's intention in creating this ambiguous situation? Write your views on this topic, quoting or making close textual reference to the play in support of your argument.

Russell presents Linda as being stuck in the working-class life of poverty. She therefore is a doomed character, similar to her mother-in-law.

The Narrator

Russell presents the Narrator as the most unusual character in *Blood Brothers*. He plays many roles and has several functions in the play. Apart from appearing as the Narrator he also takes on the roles of: milkman; gynaecologist; bus conductor; Edward's teacher; Mickey's teacher; rifle range man; and bystander at the beach. There is also scope for him to take several other minor roles, depending on a production's director (for example policeman, judge and debt collector).

There are several functions undertaken by the Narrator in *Blood Brothers*: he tells the audience the story at key moments in the play and he links the episodic scenes together, thus helping give shape to the play. The Narrator acts like the Ancient Greek Chorus (see page 13 of this guide), explaining and commenting on key events in the play. At times he talks directly to the audience, involving them in the story and asking them to make their own judgements – for example, does Mrs Johnstone really have a heart of stone? And who do we really blame for what has happened (page 107)? The Narrator also summarises the passing of time – particularly during the teenage years of Mickey, Edward and Linda.

He appears to have no social class and therefore is outside the action and appears as an omniscient onlooker. As such he may be viewed as the embodiment of fate, a slightly sinister character. Russell uses a variety of language techniques for the Narrator – rhyming couplets, free verse and songs – which are discussed in more detail in the chapter 'Language, style and analysis' (p. 58). After telling the audience at the start of the play that the brothers die, he then constantly reminds the audience of the twins' fate. He presents the themes of fate and superstition, commenting that there is always a price to pay, a debt to be repaid. These constant reminders bring a sense of foreboding to the play and Russell also adds a feeling of evil by using the metaphor of the devil to represent fate.

Key quotation

Narrator:

Oh y' know the devil's got your number
He's never far behind you
He always knows where to find you

(Page 70)

The Narrator is the character Russell uses to explore the ideas of superstition and fate, thus creating a foreboding atmosphere that pervades the whole play. In many productions he also helps with setting up the props to help the show run smoothly. As well as being a practical help to the production, this role suggests that the Narrator may actually be arranging and controlling what is happening.

Build critical skills

Narrator:

And do we blame superstition for what came to pass?
Or could it be what we, the English, have come to know as class?

(Page 107)

How could this couplet suggest that the Narrator actually has a social conscience?

In some ways the Narrator's characters can be viewed as symbolising the negative voices of various social institutions – all of which, Russell suggests, are unfair, prejudiced and hypocritical:

- At first the milkman won't listen to Mrs Johnstone's pleas, but once she is in her new home he is pleasant and flirtatious.
- The gynaecologist has no time for the difficulties Mrs Johnstone will face with two more mouths to feed instead of just one and quickly moves on to his next patient (page 10).
- The bus conductor is unsympathetic, while the judge gives Sammy a more lenient sentence because he fancies Mrs Johnstone.

- Edward's teacher appears homophobic and takes the side of Edward's bullying classmates (page 65), while Mickey's teacher lacks patience, handles Mickey's boredom badly and doesn't even bother to answer Mickey's (justified) questions.
- It is Russell's presentation of the policeman that best illustrates the difference in the attitude of the law towards the working classes and the middle classes; the policeman treats the working-class boy's actions as a 'serious crime' (page 47), while the middle-class boy's actions are simply viewed as boyish games (page 48).

At the beginning of the play the Narrator tells the audience that they are going to hear the story of the Johnstone twins who died on the same day, and at the end of the play he poses the question: who or what was responsible for their deaths? This question is at the very heart of *Blood Brothers*.

Minor characters

Sammy

At the start of the play Russell presents Sammy as an aggressive, antisocial ten-year-old who is hero-worshipped by his younger brother, Mickey. Even before the audience sees him on stage they are told that he bullies Mickey and has stolen Mickey's gun (page 31). Although Russell gives no explanation for Sammy's criminal behaviour, other than his lack of employment, the audience is told about Sammy falling out of a window when he was very young and needing to have a metal plate put in his head. Russell makes a joke about this between Mickey and Edward but we are left to wonder if this could be a reason for his aggressiveness. The incident also highlights the problems Mrs Johnstone faced, bringing up a large family as a single mother, relying on the older children to look after the young ones.

In the incident on the bus and the burning of the school, Russell demonstrates that Sammy is out of control and it is no surprise that he embarks on a life of crime. He has no job, no money and no outlet for his frustrations. He seems to have a fascination with guns, which leads to the fatalities at the end of the play; it is the gun Sammy uses in the hold-up at the petrol station that, while being held by Mickey, accidently goes off, killing Edward.

Russell uses Sammy as a catalyst in the play as he is instrumental in Mickey's downfall, being a bad influence on his younger brother. He may also be viewed as a symbol of the disaffected youth who saw no future for themselves due to government policies at the time Russell wrote the play.

Build critical skills

For what dramatic purposes does Russell create the role of Sammy?

Mr Lyons

Mr Lyons is presented as a wealthy businessman who, as the play opens, spends long periods of time working away from home. This enables the deception that Edward is his biological child to take place. Later he becomes the managing director of the factory that employs Mickey and it is he who makes Mickey redundant. Russell presents him as a rather remote figure, more concerned with making money than with the welfare of his family. He appears to have very old-fashioned, traditional values, seeing his role to be providing the money and home for the family, while leaving the upbringing of Edward to Mrs Lyons. He can be quite unsympathetic to his wife at times. Russell does present a brief tableau of domestic 'bliss' in the Lyons household, but this is soon ended by Mr Lyons getting up to go to work, despite his wife's protestations that he should be spending more time with his son (page 34). This short incident shows the audience where his priorities lie, and it's not with his family!

Build critical skills

For what dramatic purposes does Russell create the role of Mr Lyons?

Russell presents Mr Lyons as a symbol of capitalism, who appears indifferent to the lives of the workers directly under his control. He sends out heartless redundancy letters, absolving himself from any responsibility, blaming the economic situation (pages 88–90). Even Miss Jones, his faithful secretary of many years, is dismissed – and has to write her own redundancy letter!

Build critical skills

In your view, is Russell using irony in Mr Lyons' refrain 'sign of the times' to criticise capitalism? Mr Lyons, a symbol of capitalism, blames the level of unemployment on factors that he says are beyond his control. Perhaps Russell is saying that capitalism itself is at fault and that it is a sign of the times that capitalism is regarded as the only possible system in England?

GRADE BOOSTER

Turn to the 'Top quotations' section on page 94 of this guide for short, memorable quotes on the main characters. You will find it useful to have them at your fingertips in the examination.

GRADE BOOSTER

Always remember that the characters in the play have been created by a writer and that your focus needs to be on the ways the writer has made the characters come alive for the audience. Don't write about the characters as if they were real people. If the words 'Russell' or 'the writer' don't appear several times in your answer, you are probably not answering the question and are unlikely to achieve high marks.

GRADE *FOCUS*

Grade 5

To achieve Grade 5, you will develop a clear understanding of how and why Russell uses language, form and structure to create characters, supported by appropriate references to the text.

Grade 8

To achieve Grade 8, you will examine and evaluate the ways that Russell uses language, form and structure to create characters, supported by carefully chosen and well-integrated references to the text.

REVIEW YOUR LEARNING

(Answers are given on pages 98–99.)

1. In what different ways can characters be revealed to us by a writer?
2. List three adjectives that could be used to describe Mrs Johnstone and three to describe Mrs Lyons. Explain what these adjectives imply about these two characters.
3. When is the happiest time in Mickey's life?
4. From their first meeting, list three ways Russell suggests that Edward's upbringing has been different from Mickey's.
5. How does Russell show that Linda, as a child, is fond of Mickey?
6. Why does Edward not reveal his true feelings for Linda until it is too late?
7. List five roles played by the Narrator in *Blood Brothers*.
8. List three other roles he could also play, if required.
9. What might Sammy be said to represent?
10. Of what might Mr Lyons be said to be a symbol?

Themes

Target your thinking

- What is a theme? (**AO2**)
- What are the main themes of *Blood Brothers*? (**AO2**)
- What is a motif? (**AO2**)
- What are the main motifs used in *Blood Brothers*? (**AO2**)

Themes

In literature, a theme is an idea that a writer explores through language, form and structure. A theme raises questions in the minds of the audience or reader. It is usually something that the writer wants you to think about. It might appear in an examination question as 'ideas about'. Sometimes writers want you to explore what you think about a particular theme. They may pose questions rather than offering answers. In some instances, however, writers may hope that as a result of thinking about a particular theme, audience members may change their attitudes and even their behaviour.

Remember that in *Blood Brothers* Russell is creating the events in order to get his ideas across to the reader or audience; it's these ideas you should be writing about in your exam, not just the events themselves. To see *Blood Brothers* as a simple musical with lots of songs would be to miss Russell's purpose in writing the play.

The key themes and ideas in *Blood Brothers* are all linked to social class and how social/environmental forces shape people's lives. The key themes may be said to be:

- Nature vs nurture
- Class division
- Fate and superstition
- Friendship and growing up
- Love and marriage
- Education.

These ideas are all closely connected and intertwined with each other. Perhaps we could say that Russell wants us to consider whether social forces determine people's lives more than fate or our inborn nature.

GRADE BOOSTER

Showing you understand the significance of the themes that exist in the play and how they are interconnected will help you gain the highest levels. Always justify your opinion of the relative importance of these themes with quotations and keep in mind Russell's purposes in writing the play.

Nature vs nurture

Identical twins who are separated at birth are ideal subjects for social scientists who want to compare the extent to which a person's life is determined by their inherited genes and how much is determined by their upbringing and environment. As Mickey and Eddie have the same genetic make-up, the different ways their lives develop can only be due to their environment, including their upbringing and the influence of society on them. Russell uses the device of twins separated at birth to demonstrate the powerful influence of upbringing and position in society.

In an interview in *Woman's Own* magazine in 1987, the then-prime minister, Margaret Thatcher, stated that people who are out of work were 'casting their problems on society and who is society?' She then went on to say that if their 'children have a problem, [they say] it is society that is at fault', but Mrs Thatcher then stated that 'There is no such thing as society.' Her government's attitude was that everyone who worked hard could achieve whatever they wanted, irrespective of any environmental factors. Russell questions that theory in *Blood Brothers*: in the play 'nurture', not 'nature', appears to be responsible for who we are, and our place in society is vital in determining who we become.

After clearly establishing their identical natures, Russell shows the effect that seven years' upbringing in totally different environments has had on the boys. While the first meeting of the boys, aged seven, establishes their similar personalities in that they quickly become friends, it also highlights their differences. Mickey is described as being bored while Edward is described as being bright and alert (page 27). Russell suggests that Mickey is suspicious when first meeting Edward and is surprised when his demand for a sweet is met with kindness. This is in stark contrast to Edward's politeness, openness and generosity. Having a brother like Sammy who would first wee on any sweet before he gave it away, and having to ask continually for a sweet but still not getting one (page 28), unsurprisingly makes Mickey cautious and suspicious about everything.

Key quotation

Mickey: *I could have been … I could have been him!*
(Page 106)

Build critical skills

The twins' different speech patterns immediately highlight their different upbringings (see pages 59–60 of this guide). How does the incident when Mickey whispers the 'F' word to Edward illustrate the difference between their upbringings?

Build critical skills

How do you think Russell's comments on family life link to his general criticism of society?

Class division

To demonstrate his belief that environmental factors have a far greater influence than genetic factors, Russell has to have the separated twins growing up in vastly different social classes. Edward is raised in a relatively calm but emotionally cool household, whereas – despite their chaotic home life – the Johnstones do show deep bonds between family members. The friendship between characters from two very different social classes lies at the heart of the play.

As well as contrasting the two families to highlight their differences, Russell also focuses on the everyday life and difficulties faced by the poorer members of society and their attempts to survive with little money, large families, single parents, never-ending creditors, buying on hire purchase, living on unemployment benefit, and petty crime.

Russell shows, however, that money itself doesn't buy happiness: Mrs Lyons has money, but she is unable to have a child, fails to find contentment and eventually has a nervous breakdown. If money can't buy happiness, though, it *can* buy power. Russell shows how wealth and status bring privilege, even down to the way the law treats the boys.

Key quotation

Policeman (to Mrs Johnstone): *And he was about to commit a serious crime…*
(Page 47)

Policeman (to Mr Lyons): *…as I say, it was more of a prank, really…*
(Page 48)

The audience are first introduced to the class divide when Mrs Johnstone goes to work for Mrs Lyons. The difference in their social class is highlighted by their difference in language (see pages 59–60 of this guide), the cleaning props carried by Mrs Johnstone and presumably the clothes they wear. Russell also highlights their difference in social class by having Mrs Johnstone working for Mrs Lyons. While Mrs Lyons is obviously wealthy, Russell emphasises Mrs Johnstone's poverty by the number of people who come calling, either looking to be paid or to take away goods because she hasn't kept up the payments. The first meeting between Mickey and Edward also reveals the gulf in class that is emerging between the two, even at the tender age of seven. Mickey is initially suspicious of Edward's openness and is trying to find out what the trick is (page 28) when offered a sweet. Russell contrasts Mickey's use of slang language with Edward's more sophisticated language in order to bring out their class difference:

Mickey: Cos me mam says.

Edward: Well, my mummy doesn't allow me to play down here actually.

(Page 27)

Edward leads a sheltered life while Mickey already knows swear words – although not their meaning – which is a source of humour for the audience. When Edward tries to use these words to his mother, she instinctively hits him and reveals her distaste for working-class people (page 36).

When Sammy arrives he immediately, and succinctly, indicates the huge social divide that exists between people of the Johnstones' class and those of the Lyons' class, saying contemptuously that Edward is one of the posh people (page 31).

Through the boys' schooling, Russell reveals the difference that class makes in educational achievement and, as a result, career choice. Mickey's secondary modern school is boring and serves no useful purpose (page 66). In contrast, Edward is looking forward to going to one of the most prestigious universities in the country. Mickey ends up in a dead-end job in a factory, which leads only to unemployment, while Edward walks into a senior management position in the same factory and becomes a man of influence, a local councillor. Being twins, the boys have the same innate intelligence – Russell seems to be suggesting that it is the class division in society alone that produces these extreme, unfair lifestyles.

The importance of this class division is further emphasised by Russell through the Narrator, who at the end of the play asks the audience to consider whether the tragic events of the play could be caused by 'what we, the English, have come to know as class' (page 107).

Fate and superstition

All the characters, at one time or another, seem to be at the mercy of fate, whether they are superstitious or not. Due to the nature of the play (in that the ending is seen by the audience right at the beginning of the play) it may seem that the characters have no control over their destiny – much as in an Ancient Greek tragedy. The role of the all-knowing Narrator, as we have seen, is crucial in emphasising this aspect of the play. If Russell is implying, however, that the characters have no control over their destiny, then it is essential to realise that his message is not about some devil or abstract malign force controlling us, but about how the society we have created affects, dominates and controls the lives of its citizens.

Build critical skills

Could there be a deeper meaning to the recurrent idea of there being a 'price to pay'? On the surface the phrase clearly refers to a price to be paid by the mothers and the boys for the separation of the twins at birth. Could Russell, however, also be referring to the price society itself has to pay? Thinking about the context of the play, what do you think this price could be?

It is not fate that makes Mrs Johnstone give away her baby, however, but financial necessity. Her husband has left her because she has aged so much due to having so many children and so little money. Mickey gets only a dead-end job and then becomes unemployed because of the failings of the educational system and the economic policies of the country. He has the same intelligence as Edward but society has given Edward all the advantages in life. The feisty Linda has also been beaten down by poverty and towards the end of the play is looking tired and worn out (page 98). She is becoming like her mother-in-law – old before her time. Russell seems to be asking us to consider whether there really is such a thing as fate. When Mrs Lyons has her breakdown and tries to stab Mrs Johnstone, she thinks that fate is against her and that she is doomed never to escape from Mrs Johnstone. The audience, however, may view this as a simple coincidence when the Johnstone family are moved to the country. Ironically, if Mrs Lyons had remained where she was, she would soon have been free of Mrs Johnstone when the council re-housed the Johnstone family.

Key quotation

Mrs Johnstone: Oh God, Mrs Lyons, never put new shoes on a table…
(Page 9)

Superstition is a driving force in the play and underpins many of its main themes and events. Early in the play we become aware that Mrs Johnstone is very superstitious when she is shocked by Mrs Lyons putting new shoes on the table as, according to Mrs Johnstone, something bad might happen (page 9). The Narrator then reinforces the idea by mentioning several superstitions – all of which are symbols of misfortune and add to the atmosphere of foreboding in the play.

When Mrs Johnstone wants to take back her baby, Mrs Lyons exploits her superstitious nature by informing her of the curse of twins who are parted at birth learning about each other's existence.

Build critical skills

Do you think Mrs Lyons is referring to a real curse or is she simply taking advantage of Mrs Johnstone's superstitious nature in order to keep the baby? Do you think Mrs Lyons actually believes in the superstition at this point in the play? Does her attitude towards fate and superstition change at any time?

When Mrs Lyons calls her husband home from work because Edward is outside playing and no longer in her sight, the audience sees that her protective attitude towards her son has become obsessive. The first signs of a mental breakdown appear: her undefined fear and desire to move away. It is at this point that she knocks the shoes off the table (page 45), clearly now believing in the superstition. Russell is perhaps suggesting that superstitions are in fact all in the mind and not some external force controlling our lives.

At the end of the play the Narrator does ask if superstition is to blame for what has happened, but Russell also gives us an alternative cause – class.

Friendships and growing up

Mickey and Edward bond almost immediately, despite their different backgrounds and the objections of their mothers, who obviously want to keep their identities secret. This close friendship is not surprising considering they are identical twins. Russell may be suggesting here that friendships can cross social boundaries. Their friendship grows as time passes and includes Linda, who has looked out for Mickey since he was little and who, in their teenage years, continually embarrasses him by saying how much she loves him.

The friendship between the three of them adds humour to the play and, for a short time, lightens the mood. Linda often takes the lead in their games and proves herself at least equal to the boys in their activities. When they try to shoot at the statue of Peter Pan (page 43) only Linda hits the statue, and it's her quick thinking that prevents them being arrested by the policeman. But even in their happiest teenage moments Russell, through the Narrator, brings in an undercurrent of foreboding:

Narrator:

But leave them alone, let them go and play

They care not for what's at the end of the day.

(Page 82)

The relationship between Mickey, Edward and Linda has the potential for conflict, especially as Mickey and Edward are likely to be attracted to the same girl. Their boyhood friendship is so strong, however, that Edward doesn't attempt to take Linda away from Mickey and in fact actively encourages Mickey to ask her out. Although all three are so close, Linda never seems to waver in her devotion to Mickey.

The first cracks in Mickey and Edward's relationship may seem to appear when Edward is about to go to university. He encourages Mickey to finally ask Linda out, but when Mickey and Linda kiss Edward decides to leave rather than go with them to a dance at the club. He turns to go and the audience can sense the sadness he feels since he himself is in love with

Key quotation

Mickey: *Since you left I've been walking around all day, every day, lookin' for a job.* (Page 91)

her. Mickey is totally unaware of this tension and vows to work extra hard in order to pay for a Christmas party for them all (page 87). Ironically, he is made redundant shortly after this.

Edward's return at Christmas signals the end of their friendship. Mickey is dejected as he has no job and hence no money and is in no mood for Edward's jollity. Mickey has been desperately looking for a job while Edward has been having a great time at university and has been to many parties (page 91).

Because he has been financially secure all his life Edward has no appreciation of Mickey's situation and when he tries to give Mickey some money, Mickey is insulted and ends their friendship by throwing the money to the ground and telling Edward in no uncertain terms to go away (page 92). Mickey dismisses the blood brothers idea as 'kids' stuff', stating that he has had to grow up while Edward has remained a kid. Russell may be suggesting here that in the adult word, friendship is more dependent on shared experiences and that Mickey and Edward are now worlds apart in their experience of life.

Linda uses their childhood friendship, and Edward's love for her, to get Mickey a job once he is released from prison, and a house for the family. Whether her relationship with Edward goes beyond friendship is up to the reader/audience to decide.

Love and marriage

Russell portrays several different kinds of love in *Blood Brothers*: the love of a mother for her children, the romantic and sexual love of young people, and the supportive (and unsupportive) love within a marriage.

Despite her difficulties, Mrs Johnstone is determined to prevent Social Services from taking her children away from her. She loves them all intensely (page 11). Ironically, it is her love for her yet-unborn twins that allows her to give one away to Mrs Lyons: she sees a better future for a child brought up in a middle-class family. We know very little about the love between Mr and Mrs Johnstone – there certainly seems to have been a strong physical attraction between them and Mrs Johnstone was certainly flattered to be compared to Marilyn Monroe. What love he had for her, however, didn't last once she had lost her figure, and he left her for a younger woman. Mrs Lyons also loves her (adopted) son but is over-protective and smothers him with her love, which ultimately becomes a destructive love that leads to the death of both twins.

Mickey and Edward both fall in love with Linda, who has had a crush on Mickey since childhood. Out of respect for his blood brother, though, Edward refrains from declaring his love for Linda, although he comes very close to it in his song on page 85. When he has come back on holiday from university and been rejected by Mickey, however, he does ask Linda to marry him, but of course Linda has married Mickey while Edward was away at university and is expecting his baby. She admits to loving Edward, though.

When Linda turns to him for help after Mickey has been released from prison and is suffering from depression, it is natural that Edward will help her – but do they actually have an affair?

As a wife, Linda supports Mickey, trying her best to wean him off the drugs and actually compromising herself to get them a home and Mickey a job. The strain of her marriage and life of poverty has aged her beyond her years.

Russell presents Mr Lyons as supporting his wife financially but as being rather cold and unsupportive emotionally towards her, being more interested in his job than in his family. It seems that he agreed to the move into the country in order to placate his wife rather than from any real concern for her well-being. Ironically, he will not entertain the idea of satisfying his wife's desire for a child by adoption. Most of their marriage therefore is based on the deception that Mr Lyons is Edward's natural father.

Key quotation

Linda: *I suppose, I suppose I always … loved you, in a way.* (Page 94)

Education

The theme of education is intrinsically linked to Russell's criticism of society and social class. Russell shows us that wealth and social standing bring many educational opportunities, which children from working-class backgrounds could not hope to attain.

Although the difference in attitude to learning is made clear in the first meeting between Mickey and Edward, when Mickey doesn't know what a dictionary is, it is their formal schooling that creates the unbridgeable gap between the boys and determines their career paths. One goes to university and has a successful career in politics, while the other has a boring factory job making boxes, followed by redundancy and depression. The audience are likely therefore to see Mickey's drug addiction and crime in a more sympathetic light.

In the scene in Mickey's school Russell seems to be criticising state education in **secondary modern schools** of the time. Mickey and the whole class are bored. Mickey questions the value of their education when he sarcastically states that it will help him get a job if he knows what pygmies in Africa eat (page 67). We know nothing specific about Edward's education in the private school but we do know that his school has prepared him for university and therefore for much better career opportunities. Russell presents both boys' teachers as bullies who are uninterested in their students.

Secondary modern schools: mid-twentieth century schools for pupils who were deemed to be less academically able, based on the results of a single test that children took at age 11. Secondary moderns came to be regarded as offering a vastly inferior, rather than an alternative, form of education.

Build critical skills

How do you think Russell's criticism of the educational system links to his views on nature vs nurture as presented in *Blood Brothers*?

The education system as Russell presents it also shapes the lives of the female characters. Like Mickey, Linda has no career prospects. She appears to have no option but to become a housewife and is soon worn down by the cares that poverty brings. Mrs Johnstone's lack of education means that she had no means of escape from poverty once her husband left her. She is capable of only low-paid, unskilled work and is reliant on the State for her family's housing. Mrs Lyons, even with her presumably middle-class education, is also dependent on her husband rather than being self-reliant.

Could Russell be suggesting that the traditional lives women were expected to lead at this time encouraged them to lack ambition and to be reliant on a male figure – and also that the traditional educational system was failing to address this issue?

Motifs

An important stylistic feature used by Russell in *Blood Brothers* is the use of motifs. A motif is a recurring idea, feature or symbol that reinforces a theme, tells us more about a character or prepares us for what will happen later in the play. Of the several motifs in *Blood Brothers*, perhaps the most important is that of the actress Marilyn Monroe.

▲ Marilyn Monroe

Marilyn Monroe

Marilyn Monroe was a very famous Hollywood actress whose image was (and still is) well known, even to people who did not watch her films. She was presented by the media as a kind of 'perfect' fantasy woman and she appeared to live a glamorous and carefree lifestyle, even being a close, personal friend of the President of the United States. She was the envy of women and the dream girl for every man – the epitome of Hollywood glamour. She was a true iconic figure. The reality of her life, however, was very different: she had a string of broken marriages and became dependent on antidepressants. Marilyn mostly grew up with foster parents, although she lived briefly with her mother before her mother was put into a hospital suffering from 'mental instability'. Marilyn even spent some time in an orphanage. The fostering/adoption link and the fact that Marilyn's real mother, like Mrs Lyons, was mentally unstable may be the reason Russell chose to use Marilyn as a motif in the play. Marilyn eventually died from an overdose of pills in 1962, when only 36 years old.

There are fourteen references to Marilyn Monroe at eight separate points in the play, showing how significant this motif is. At each of these points Russell refers to a different aspect of her life and public image. The use of this motif helps to place the play firmly in its historical context. It also creates a contrast between the glamour of Hollywood movie stars and the poverty of the Johnstone family.

The first reference to this motif is at the very beginning of the play when Mrs Johnstone enters singing about how she met her husband, who told her that she was more sexy than Marilyn Monroe (page 5) and on their wedding day people said that she was more lovely than Marilyn Monroe (page 6). At first Mrs Johnstone enjoys the glamour of Monroe's public image but this backfires as her husband refuses to go dancing with her when she becomes pregnant again and looks much less attractive than Marilyn Monroe, and eventually he leaves her for another Marilyn Monroe lookalike (page 6). Mrs Johnstone picks up the motif soon afterwards when she tells her hungry children that she is getting a job next week and they will all live the high life, just like Marilyn Monroe (pages 7–8).

Act Two also begins with positive images of Marilyn Monroe as the glamorous sex symbol. The Johnstone family have moved and life is improving – Mrs Johnstone has become friendly with the milkman (she is now able to pay her bills on time) who compares her legs to Marilyn Monroe's (page 59). Even the judge gives Sammy a lenient sentence because Mrs Johnstone reminded him of Marilyn Monroe (page 60). As a sign of Mickey growing up, Mrs Johnstone informs the audience that her son (now aged fourteen) has reached puberty and is dreaming of pretty girls like Marilyn Monroe (page 60).

There then follows, however, the first negative reference to Marilyn Monroe's life. Mrs Johnstone hopes that Edward will be all right, unlike Marilyn Monroe (page 61). This reference to Marilyn Monroe creates an element of foreboding as the audience will know that Marilyn Monroe died a tragic death at the young age of 36. Edward, like her, appears to have a brilliant future ahead before tragically losing his life at an early age.

Later in the play, once Mickey has been sent to prison, Russell creates a close parallel between his and Marilyn Monroe's fates when Mrs Johnstone sings that jail has sent him into depression, similar to Marilyn Monroe (page 97) and the audience then learns that Mickey has become hooked on antidepressants. This is compared to Monroe's own depression as she became addicted to antidepressant drugs. Mrs Johnstone's song ends with an ironic prophecy in saying that he has no feeling for life in him, that he acts as if he was dead, just as Marilyn Monroe is dead (page 98).

The final references to Marilyn Monroe are at the very end of the play, when Mrs Johnstone and the rest of the cast sing the final song before the curtain falls. Mrs Johnstone is hoping that all the events the audience have witnessed have been nothing more than a scene from an old

GRADE BOOSTER

To gain the highest grades you need to know how Russell uses the Marilyn Monroe motif and the effect it has on the audience. It is not enough just to know when the references occur.

▲ Child with gun

Marilyn Monroe film (page 107). Russell also indicates the passage of time in this song: at the start of the play Marilyn is at the height of her fame but now her movies are 'old' and 'of years ago'. The importance of the Marilyn Monroe motif is shown by the fact that the play ends with her name.

Other motifs

Other important motifs in the play are:

- Guns
- Games
- Dancing.

Guns

Initially, guns are mentioned as toys and linked to the games the children play. The first mentioned of guns is an innocent request from Mrs Johnstone's 'kids' for an 'air pistol', among other items (page 19). Then Mickey, aged seven, comes home carrying a 'toy gun' to find the door locked – his mother is hiding from the rent man. The first symbolic reference to guns is when his mother unlocks the door and Mickey complains that his brother, Sammy, has taken his best gun (page 24). The reference to Sammy stealing a gun from Mickey foreshadows the failed robbery that will eventually lead to Mickey's and Edward's deaths.

Key quotation

Mickey: *Our Sammy's robbed me other gun*
(Page 24)

Build critical skills

Commenting on the significance of specific words, in this case Russell's use of the word 'robbed' (foreshadowing the failed robbery of the petrol station and giving us an insight into Sammy's character) is an important skill that will help you gain high marks.

Shortly afterwards, Sammy appears on stage for the first time and almost immediately states that soon he is going to get a real gun (page 31), again foreshadowing future events.

The 'kids games' outwardly portray the children playing innocent games, linked to TV and cinema films. The fact that the children don't understand the meaning of death is shown by how they can count to ten then come 'alive' again when they have been shot.

The whole section takes on a sinister meaning, however, as we know that life is not just a game, as Mickey will find out to his cost. (Remember, the audience has already seen the final moments of the play – the deaths of Mickey and Edward.) Russell does show that toy guns are not just for working-class boys – when Edward's father comes home, he gives Edward a toy gun.

The next time a gun is seen is when Mickey, Edward and Linda are shooting at the statue of Peter Pan in the park with Sammy's air pistol. Only Linda hits the target. Then at the fairground, aged fifteen, the three teenagers try their luck at the rifle range but Linda this time misses with all three shots, much to the boys' amazement. As the scene freezes, with Linda the middle one of a piggy-in-the-middle game, the Narrator picks up the rifle and asks the audience who will tell her 'The price she'll pay for just being there?' (page 82). By missing with her shots this time, in contrast to when they were younger, could Russell be hinting that Linda's life is doomed to failure, just like Mrs Johnstone's?

When Edward moves away, he gives Mickey a 'goodbye' present – a toy gun (page 51), ironically foreshadowing later events.

The undercurrent of violence comes to the surface with the killing of the petrol-station attendant by Sammy. The narrator at this point refers back to the childhood games but now it's for real, it's not a game and there is no counting to ten to come back alive.

The gun that Sammy hides under the floorboards is the same gun that Mickey uses to shoot Edward. Although Mickey is desperate and cannot control his rage (page 106), the actual killing of Edward is accidental – Mickey is waving his gun hand at Edward when the gun accidentally goes off and kills Edward. The police open fire, killing Mickey (page 107).

GRADE BOOSTER

To gain high grades you should understand how Russell uses the idea of guns to foreshadow the final tragic events of the play and also to create an undercurrent of violence caused by the poverty and hopelessness of the working class at this time.

Games

As we have seen, games are closely linked with guns – the games the children play are based on what they see on television and in the cinema (creating a link to Marilyn Monroe). Having the children play games enables Russell to explore childhood and show how friendships are created and developed. They also allow tragic events to be foreshadowed and indicate the passage of time.

The first reference to games is in the duet between Mrs Johnstone and Mrs Lyons where Mrs Johnstone is close to agreeing to Mrs Lyons' suggestion that she give up one of the twins. One of the arguments

Key quotation

Mickey: *See, this means that we're blood brothers, an' that we always have to stand by each other.*
(Page 30)

Key quotation

Linda: *Leave him alone!*
(Page 41)

advanced by Mrs Lyons is that the twin would have a much more comfortable upbringing with lots of toys and a nice garden to play in (page 13).

It is through playing 'cowboys and Indians' near the big houses when Mickey is seven that he is first seen by Edward, who comes out to meet him. They then quickly become friends and blood brothers.

The importance of the 'kids games' section has been seen in relation to guns but it is also the first time that Linda appears, protecting Mickey from the taunts of Sammy's gang and thus establishing their life-long relationship. Ironically, however, Russell later shows us how she can't protect Mickey in real life. It is during this game that Mickey cries because he doesn't 'wanna die.' Russell's use of dramatic irony in Linda's reply – that when Mickey dies he will see his twin again (page 42) – is very effective here, creating a sense of foreboding in the audience.

The games change as time passes – the imaginary shooting of Indians with toy guns by seven-year-olds is replaced by teenagers shooting at the rifle range with real guns. There is a very dramatic, symbolic moment when Russell freezes the action with Linda the middle one of a piggy-in-the-middle game with Mickey and Edward. As we have seen, the Narrator picks up the rifle and asks the audience 'Who'd tell the girl in the middle of the pair / The price she'll pay for just being there?' (page 82). The foreshadowing of Linda's later relationship with Edward and how she is torn between her feelings for the two twins is clear for the audience to see in this freezeframe of the game.

As we have also seen, when Sammy shoots the petrol-station attendant, Russell links the scene back to childhood games by having Sammy tell the attendant that this is for real and is not a game (page 95).

The final reference to games is in the finale with Mrs Johnstone's song asking someone to tell her that all that has happened has only been a game and that they can start all over again (page 107). This reinforces her unwillingness to accept the fact that both her twins have died in such tragic circumstances.

GRADE BOOSTER

To help improve your level, remember to use quotations to support your comments on the function of Russell's use of the games motif.

Dancing

The final motif employed by Russell is the concept of dancing. This motif is usually used to represent courtship, happy and carefree times, sexual pleasure, and escape from the realities and drudgeries of everyday life.

At the beginning of the play Mrs Johnstone sings of how she met her husband at a dance and they went dancing together. When she became pregnant they married but still went dancing. When she became pregnant for a second time, however, her husband wouldn't go dancing with her anymore as she was less attractive (page 6). Her husband eventually walked out on her for a younger woman and it's now they who go dancing leaving Mrs Johnstone to bring up their seven children (with the twins still to come) alone.

▲ A 1960s dance hall

At the end of Act One, when Mrs Johnstone hears about the council's decision to relocate the family to a nicer area, she fantasises about a return to happier days where a man might take her dancing again (pages 56–57) and feels that she is so happy she could dance. At first, life does seem to improve for Mrs Johnstone, as at the beginning of Act Two she tells us that Joe, the milkman, sometimes takes her dancing (page 59) and that Mickey is starting to grow up, dreaming of girls who look like Marilyn Monroe and dancing in secret (page 60). When Edward starts to express his feelings for Linda he says to her that if he was Mickey he would ask her to dance (page 85).

The dancing motif takes on a more negative connotation, however, when Edward, about to go university, turns down the offer of going to the dance with Mickey and Linda because he now feels left out as Mickey has finally been persuaded to ask Linda out – by Edward himself, ironically.

GRADE BOOSTER

To help improve your grade, remember to comment on the two different, contrasting uses of the dancing motif when exploring its function in the play.

The motif becomes even more sinister when Mickey tells Linda to get dressed up because they are going out dancing (page 95). He plans to get the money by helping Sammy rob the petrol station. Although Linda does not know his plans, she is (rightly) fearful for him.

The final use of the dancing motif concerns Mickey. Russell uses the motif ironically in that instead of representing happy, carefree times he uses it to show how Mickey is unable to cope in prison: he needs antidepressant drugs to calm him down as his mind is dancing all over the place. When Mickey is released from prison he is a changed man; he looks older and his speech is slower due to his medication. There are now no happy times, no going out dancing with Linda (pages 97–98).

GRADE BOOSTER

Make sure you know all the key themes of the play well. Test yourself on these themes by talking about them, by writing them down without the help of your text or by planning responses to some questions in timed conditions.

GRADE *FOCUS*

Grade 5

To achieve Grade 5, you will reveal a clear understanding of the key themes of the play and how Russell uses language, form and structure to explore them, supported by appropriate references to the text.

Grade 8

To achieve Grade 8, you will be able to examine and evaluate the key themes of the play, analysing the ways that Russell uses language, form and structure to explore them. Comments will be supported by carefully chosen and well-integrated references to the text.

REVIEW YOUR LEARNING

(Answers are given on page 99.)

1. What do we mean when we talk about the themes of a play?
2. List two main themes of *Blood Brothers*.
3. Why do you think it is important for Russell's message that Mickey and Edward are identical twins and not just brothers?
4. When are the audience first introduced to the idea of a class divide in society?
5. What are the first signs of the importance of superstition in the play? List four superstitions that appear in the play.
6. What do you think is Russell's message regarding the influence of fate in our lives?
7. How does Russell show that the education system fails Mickey?
8. What is a motif?
9. List four examples of how Russell uses the motif of Marilyn Monroe.
10. What other motifs does Russell use in the play?

Language, style and analysis

Target your thinking

- How does Russell tell the story of *Blood Brothers* to his audience? (**AO2**)
- What techniques does he use to make the staging of *Blood Brothers* effective? (**AO1**, **AO2**)
- How does Russell use dialogue in the play? (**AO2**, **AO3**)

You will notice from the questions above that when analysing language and style the Assessment Objective with which we are most concerned is AO2. AO2 refers to the writer's methods and is usually highlighted in exam questions by the word 'how'. (Note: AO2 is not assessed by Edexcel in this section.)

Examiners report that AO2 is often the Assessment Objective most overlooked by students in the examination. Candidates who fail to address AO2 often write about the characters in a play as if they are real people involved in real events rather than analysing them as 'constructs' or creations of the writer.

To succeed at AO2, you must deal effectively with the writer's use of language, form and structure. Form and language are discussed below; turn to page 23 of this guide for an analysis of the structure of *Blood Brothers*.

Form

There are certain dramatic conventions associated with the play form, and *Blood Brothers* conforms to these. They include stage directions, sets, stage props, music and, of course, dialogue. The decisions that a playwright makes about all these different aspects are closely related to both the structure and the language of the play.

Stage directions

Stage directions are extremely important in a production of a play as they convey the author's ideas to the actors and hence to the audience. Most of the stage directions in *Blood Brothers* are fairly straightforward but sometimes they are used for a very specific dramatic effect. Thus, the most significant stage direction comes at the very beginning of the play – the re-enactment of the final moments of the play. Elsewhere, the apparent idyllic setting of the Lyons' home is conveyed through mime and stage directions (page 34), while the reality of their family life is conveyed through the subsequent dialogue between Mr and Mrs Lyons. As discussed on page 30 of this guide, Russell's most dramatic use of stage directions is when Mrs Lyons points out Linda and Edward to Mickey.

Significance of the set

Some authors are very specific on set details to be used in a production of their play. J.B. Priestley, for example, gives quite detailed instructions on how the opening set of *An Inspector Calls* should look. Other authors give free rein to a director regarding set design. In his Production Note for *Blood Brothers* (page 2), Russell gives an indication of how the set should appear on stage. It should be an open stage with only two semi-permanent areas: the Lyons house Upper Left of the stage and the Johnstone house Down Right of the stage. Although we see the interior of the Lyons' affluent home, the audience usually sees only the exterior door of the Johnstone home. The areas in between are used for street scenes, etc. The overall effect must be for the play to flow smoothly with no cumbersome scene changes. Lighting can be used to indicate different settings and time spans as well as to signify where the focus of the action is to take place. There should be minimal props and furniture.

Language

A playwright's use of language is very different to that of an author in a novel. Dialogue in a novel may be important but usually plays a secondary role to the third person narrative, while in a play the spoken word *is* the play!

Dialect and Received Pronunciation

The most noticeable effect of Russell's use of language is how it reveals the difference between the working-class characters and the middle-class characters. The working-class characters (e.g. Mrs Johnstone, Mickey, Sammy and Linda) speak with a working-class Liverpool dialect, while the middle-class characters (e.g. Mr and Mrs Lyons and Edward) speak in Standard English with **Received Pronunciation**. This difference in spoken language highlights one of the main themes of the play – the importance of class in society.

As well as highlighting this major theme of the play (see page 44 of this guide), Russell uses the differences in language, and the understanding of language, to add humour to *Blood Brothers*. Mickey's first words betray his working-class upbringing (see page 24).

Key quotation

Mickey: *Cos me mam says.*

Edward: *Well, my mummy doesn't allow me to play down here actually.*

(Page 27)

Received Pronunciation: the accent that is associated with the educated middle classes, the accent of the elite in society, although it is only one of many accents in Britain.

Build critical skills

Some audiences in the 1980s were shocked by the use of the 'F' word in the play. Is its use justified? Does this use of 'taboo' language have the same impact now?

When the twins first meet, Edward is fascinated by the language Mickey uses (page 28) and is in awe of him when he tells Edward that he knows the 'F' word – even though Mickey doesn't know what it means! Their difference in upbringing and education is then clearly shown when Edward says he'll look up the word in the dictionary – a thing Mickey hasn't even heard of. There then follows a lovely, humorous conversation about the plate in Sammy's head, where Russell again shows Mickey's working-class upbringing as he does not know what a side plate is. This play on words is repeated when the boys go to the cinema to learn about sex (page 74) and Edward, overawed at what he has just seen, sings about how it's a nice way to spend the evening but replaces 'it's' with 'tits' (page 80).

Songs

The most obvious stylistic feature of *Blood Brothers* is the use of songs. In *Blood Brothers* there are twelve separate musical numbers, some of which are reprised several times (e.g. 'Marilyn Monroe' and 'Shoes Upon The Table'). The songs have several different, distinct purposes:

- **To add entertainment to the play**. All musicals are designed to have a high entertainment value.
- **To fill in the background to the action and advance the story line**. In 'Marilyn Monroe' Mrs Johnstone briefly tells us her life-story up to the start of the play: how she met her husband who eventually left her for a younger woman, and how poverty and seven children have aged her beyond her years. In 'Light Romance' she tells how the renewed friendship between Linda and Edward has developed beyond simple friendship.

▲ 'Right to work' protest march, Manchester to Liverpool, 1980

'Miss Jones' informs the audience of the economic downturn and mass unemployment that occurred during the Thatcher years. Mickey is made redundant, apparently on his wedding day, and the uncaring attitude of Mr Lyons, representing the interests of business, is demonstrated when he even sacks his secretary. Mr Lyons takes no responsibility for his actions.

- **To express and create emotion**. In 'Tell Me It's Not True' Mrs Johnstone (then the rest of the company) at the end of the play sing of their regret and disbelief at the events that have just unfolded. Their powerful emotions are shared by the audience.

  In 'Miss Jones' the people on the dole (the Dole-ites) remark with bitter irony that unemployment is simply called leisure time now (page 90).

  In 'Long Sunday Afternoon' (page 53) Mickey expresses the boredom of childhood and also how he is missing his best friend – Edward.

  In 'I'm Not Saying A Word' Edward expresses his feelings for Linda and what he would say if he was Mickey (page 84).

Key quotation

Mrs Johnstone: *Tell me it's not true, / Say it's just a story.*
(Page 107)

- **To explore character**. In 'That Guy' Mickey and Edward sing how they would each like to be like the other. As well as highlighting how their upbringings have made them different, it also serves to remind the audience that in many ways they are similar, they are identical twins.
- **To create atmosphere**. 'Shoes Upon The Table' is all about the superstitions that affect people's lives and the consequences that will result because Mrs Johnstone has 'sold a son' (page 23) – and that there is no escape from these.

  In 'Bright New Day', however, the mood is very positive and upbeat. The Johnstone family are starting a new life (page 57) and hopes are high for a better life.

Key quotation

Narrator:

Now you know the devil's got your number
He's gonna find y'
Y' know he's right behind y'

(Pages 45–46)

- **To explore motivation**. In 'My Child' Mrs Johnstone begins to see the advantages of one of the twins growing up in a middle-class family rather than in poverty. Mrs Lyons encourages her to give up a twin hence the song becomes a duet as the two women begin to reach agreement.

Key quotation

Mrs Lyons *and* **Mrs Johnstone** *(together)*: *A credit to me.*
(Page 14)

- **To serve a structural function** by linking scenes by means of reprising a song, that is, using some of the same words and tunes; and they also link the two acts, for example 'Easy Terms'.
- **To help remind the audience of the key themes**. 'Easy Terms' explores the theme of poverty – living on the dole (page 18) – and also reminds the audience of the inevitable consequences of Mrs Johnstone's actions: 'the price I'll have to pay'. The reprise of this song also uses the title phrase to refer to the fact that Mrs Johnstone is Edward's mother but will never tell him.

  'Kids Game' explores violence and death in the context of children's games, where you can become alive again simply by counting from one to ten (page 40). More importantly, it foreshadows the robbery that will send Mickey to prison and eventually to his, and Edward's, death. Sammy warns the petrol-station attendant that this is for real, not a game (page 95).

  As we have seen above, 'Miss Jones' helps to place the play in its context of mass unemployment and social unrest.

GRADE BOOSTER

To gain the highest grades you need to know how Russell uses the songs to create different dramatic effects for the audience. It is not enough just to know where each song occurs.

Note that the original version of the play did not have songs but Russell decided to add them after the success of another musical he wrote.

Humour

It is quite common in plays of a tragic nature for the playwright to use humour to relieve the tension and provide a contrast with the tragic scenes. The porter in *Macbeth* and the gravediggers in *Hamlet* are classic example of Shakespeare employing this technique. In *Blood Brothers*, Russell also uses humour in this way, highlighting some of the themes of the play and bringing out the personalities of the characters.

One use of humour by Russell is when Mickey and Edward meet for the first time and they discuss the plate in Sammy's head (page 29). Their confusion and misunderstandings reveal their childhood innocence – but also their difference in social class (see page 44 of this guide).

As the boys reach adolescence, Russell shows their sexual curiosity and awkwardness through humour when they go to get money for the cinema to learn about sex (page 74) and Mrs Johnstone joins in their fun, revealing her friendly, down-to-earth nature. The real significance of this light-hearted scene, however, is that it is immediately followed by one of the most dramatic scenes in the play – the attempted stabbing of Mrs Johnstone by Mrs Lyons. The juxtaposition of these two scenes heightens the effect of this dramatic encounter.

Elsewhere, the use of taboo language by the children, particularly its inexpert use by Edward ('You're ... you're a fuckoff!', page 36), amuses as it is both mildly shocking and at the same time hilariously innocent. Again, this is immediately and horrifyingly followed by Mrs Lyons striking her son hard, to instant sobering effect.

As well as verbal humour, Russell employs some visual humour – albeit off-stage – when the Johnstone family arrive in the countryside. Mrs Johnstone's remarks telling Sammy to get off the cow, which turns out to be a bull, and commenting on Donna-Marie stepping into something unpleasant (page 57) – conjure up a wonderful comic image of city folk in the country for the first time, as well as giving the audience another example of Sammy being out of control.

Russell shows how Linda's feistiness brings a touch of humour to the play as she plays a trick on a policeman so that the three of them can run away (page 81). This mirrors the earlier, humorous scene with the policeman when they were much younger (page 47).

Parallel scenes

Russell uses **parallel scenes** to emphasise the class differences. For example, a scene in the Johnstone household will often be followed by a scene in the Lyons household that contrasts the poverty of the Johnstone family with the middle-class values of the Lyons family (e.g. pages 60–61; see also page 24 in the 'Plot and structure' section).

Parallel scenes: where one scene in a play is followed by another that echoes it in theme or setting.

Another example is when the policeman visits Mrs Johnstone and gives her a severe warning about Mickey's behaviour, but to Mr Lyons he describes Edward's actions as merely a 'prank' (page 48), showing a clear difference in attitudes from the authorities, based solely on class (see also page 18 in the 'Plot and structure' section).

Build critical skills

Consider the parallel scenes where Mrs Johnstone tells the audience that Mickey has 'started dancing, secret dancing' (page 60), while on the other side of the stage Mrs Lyons teaches Edward the waltz. What does the contrast between Mickey's informal dancing and Edward's formal waltzing highlight about the difference in their social class?

Perhaps the clearest example of Russell's use of parallel scenes is in the classroom, where Mickey in his comprehensive school and Edward in his private school both stand up to their teachers and are suspended. These events serve to remind the audience that Mickey and Edward are identical twins with the same DNA and so can be expected to share similar qualities (pages 65–67; see also page 19 in the 'Plot and structure' section).

GRADE BOOSTER

As well as being able to identify the techniques Russell uses, you need to be able to comment on the function they play in delivering Russell's message and adding to the dramatic effect of *Blood Brothers*.

GRADE BOOSTER

It's not enough to state that the Narrator sometimes uses rhyming couplets; you need to identify *why* Russell has used this technique and be able to comment on the effect he intended to achieve.

Use of the Narrator

A rather unusual technique for a modern play is Russell's use of a Narrator (and to a certain extent, a Chorus) to comment on the action and link the scenes together. His functions and roles in the play have been dealt with in more detail in the section on 'Characterisation' (see page 37 of this guide). A noticeable feature of the language Russell chooses for him is the use of rhyming couplets, for example in the first verse of his opening address to the audience he rhymes 'twins'/'pins' and 'day'/'away' and later, when commenting on Mrs Lyons' plan to take one of the twins, 'can'/'plan' and 'room'/'womb'. One of the effects Russell achieves by using rhyming couplets is to link the play back to traditional fairy tales and nursery rhymes, so reminding the audience that this is just a story and not real, therefore enabling the audience to perhaps focus on Russell's message and themes rather than on the characters as real people. The use of this nursery-rhyme rhyming style also connects to the child-centred early part of the play. The Narrator's use of language (rhyme or free verse) helps to set him apart from the other characters and to emphasise his status as an independent observer.

Imagery

To emphasise the identical nature of the twins, right at the start of the play the Narrator uses the simile of them being as alike 'as two new pins', an image that links to traditional superstitions relating to pins.

Throughout the play Russell uses an extended metaphor comparing the price there is to pay for separating the twins with the price of buying goods on the 'never never' – the only method open to people who are living in poverty like the Johnstone family; poverty of course being the reason for the twins' separation. This comparison is most clearly seen when she sings the song 'Easy Terms' (sung to the babies before Mrs Lyons takes one, page 18), where she herself realises that she doesn't know 'the price [she'll] have to pay'. As we have seen, the Narrator brings a sense of foreboding and inevitability to the play; this effect is partly created by Russell constantly employing the metaphor of the devil getting closer and closer to represent the fatal consequences of Mrs Johnstone giving Edward away.

The innocence of the three friends (Mickey, Edward and Linda) in their teenage years, unaware of what the future will bring, is clearly revealed by Russell in his powerful image of innocent lambs that will be slaughtered (see page 82). He specifically links this image to Linda, who will be caught up in the twins' destiny: 'Who'd tell the girl in the middle of the pair / The price she'll pay for just being there?'

Pathetic fallacy: a technique whereby human emotions/ qualities are given to nature or to inanimate objects. Here, the seasons and the weather are used by Russell to emphasise the sadness of what is about to happen.

Russell uses **pathetic fallacy** to introduce the start of events that lead to the play's final denouement, as an effective method of warning the audience of the tragedy to come. The sun fades away, winter displaces summer and the rain starts to fall (page 87) – all clear indications and foreshadowing of the tragedy to come.

Dramatic irony

As the audience knows the final outcome at the start of the play, the opportunities for **dramatic irony**, to heighten the tension and increase the sense of foreboding, are many in *Blood Brothers*.

Dramatic irony: when a character says or does something, the importance of which is clear to the audience but not understood by the character.

Perhaps the clearest example of dramatic irony comes in the first meeting between Mickey and Edward, aged seven. While the boys are surprised to find out that they share the same birthday and decide to become blood brothers, the audience knows that they are real brothers.

Build critical skills

Re-read the scene where Mickey and Edward first meet (page 27). Identify any moments or comments from the twins that will cause an audience to think: *Well, we know better than that.*

Dramatic irony can also be found in the use of the Marilyn Monroe motif, where the audience would be expected to know the fate of the actress and thus to realise that linking her to Mrs Johnstone and Mickey is an ominous sign.

Mrs Lyons' comment that she believes an adopted child can come to be like one's own natural child (page 8) is heavily laced with irony as the events of the play show. Shortly after this, Mrs Johnstone reveals how she thinks she can just about scrape by with one more mouth to feed – only then to be told she is expecting twins.

Mrs Johnstone's song 'Easy Terms' is also full of dramatic irony – the audience is well aware of the final outcome and the price she will have to pay (the death of her two sons), while she is worried only by vague feelings of foreboding.

Russell even makes the simple children's games ironic: death to them is a simple matter of counting to ten then coming back to life, but the audience is well aware of the realities of death that will conclude the play.

Build critical skills

Identify further examples of dramatic irony in the play. For example look at Linda's words of comfort to Mickey on page 42. Mrs Lyons' remark to Edward about Mickey not being the same as him (page 36) is also worth considering.

Repetition

The most important use of repetition is Russell's use of the Narrator continually to build up a sense of foreboding and inevitability by his references to the devil (e.g. pages 23, 44, 45, 70, 103, 104). Russell also uses repetition by Mrs Johnstone to emphasise the same idea of foreboding and inevitability, by references to a price to be paid for her actions (e.g. her song 'Easy Terms' on pages 17–18, 102, 103).

GRADE *FOCUS*

Grade 5

To achieve Grade 5, you will show a clear understanding of the methods Russell uses to create effects for the reader, supported by appropriate references to the text.

Grade 8

To achieve Grade 8, you will explore and analyse the methods Russell uses to create effects for the reader, supported by carefully chosen and well-integrated references to the text.

REVIEW YOUR LEARNING

(Answers are given on pages 99–100.)

1. Why is it especially important in *Blood Brothers* that different characters use different dialects?
2. What technique is Russell using when he has the Narrator describe the twins as being as alike 'as two new pins' (page 5)?
3. Why are stage directions so important in a play?
4. What is the reasoning behind having an open stage with minimal props and furniture?
5. What is foreshadowing?
6. Identify an example of foreshadowing in the play.
7. Give three examples of how Russell uses the musical numbers to help convey his message.
8. What technique is being used when the Narrator speaks the quatrain (four lines) beginning 'It was one day in October…' (page 87)?
9. Name one effect of the use of rhyming couplets in the play.
10. What is dramatic irony? Give two examples of the use of dramatic irony in the play.

Tackling the exams

Target your thinking

- What sorts of questions will you have to answer?
- What is the best way to plan your answer?
- How can you improve your grade?
- What do you have to do to achieve the highest grades?

Your response to a question on *Blood Brothers* will be assessed in a 'closed book' English literature examination, which means that you are not allowed to take a copy of the play into the exam with you. Different examination boards will test you in different ways and it is vital that you know on which paper the modern prose or drama text will be, so that you can be well-prepared on the day of the examination.

Whichever board you are studying, the following table explains which paper and section the play appears in and gives you information about the sort of question you will face and how you will be assessed.

Exam board	AQA	Edexcel	WJEC Eduqas
Paper and section	Paper 2 Section A: Modern prose or drama	Paper 1 Section B: Post-1914 British play or novel	Paper 2 Section A: Post-1914 prose/drama
Type of question	One traditional essay-type question	One traditional essay-type question	One traditional essay-type question using an extract from the play as stimulus
Closed book?	Yes	Yes	Yes
Choice of question?	Yes: one question from a choice of two	Yes: one question from a choice of two	No
Paper and section length	Paper 2 = 2 hours 15 minutes Section A = approx. 40–45 minutes	Paper 1 = 1 hour 45 minutes Section B = 50 minutes	Paper 2 = 2 hours 30 minutes Section A = approx. 45–50 minutes
Percentage of whole grade	20%	25%	20%
AOs assessed	AO1, AO2, AO3, AO4	AO1, AO3, AO4	AO1, AO2, AO4
Is AO4 (SPaG) assessed in this section?	Yes	Yes	Yes

Marking

The marking of your responses varies according to the board your school or you have chosen. Each exam board has a slightly different mark scheme, consisting of a ladder of levels. The marks you achieve in each part of the examination will be converted to your final overall grade. Grades are numbered from 1 to 9, with 9 being the highest.

It is important that you familiarise yourself with the relevant mark scheme(s) for your examination. After all, how can you do well unless you know exactly what is required?

Assessment Objectives for individual assessments are explained in the next section of the guide (page 76).

Approaching the examination question

First impressions

First, read the whole question and make sure you understand *exactly* what the task requires you to do. It is very easy in the highly pressured atmosphere of the examination room to misread a question – and this can be disastrous. Under no circumstances should you try and twist the question to match the one that you have spent hours revising or the one that you did brilliantly on in your mock exam!

How to read the question

Are you being asked to think about how a character or a theme is being presented? Make sure you know so that you will be able to sustain your focus later.

Look carefully at any bullet points you are given. They are there to help and guide you.

Three exam boards offer *Blood Brothers* as a text. Two (AQA and Edexcel) use an essay-type question. WJEC Eduqas uses a format based on an extract from the play. The wordings and formats of the questions are slightly different for each board.

As a starting point, you may wish to underline keywords in the question, such as 'how' to remind you to write about methods, and any other words that you feel will help you focus on answering the question you are being asked.

Below you can see examples of the question type from each examination board, annotated in this way.

AQA

How does Russell present a divided society in *Blood Brothers*?

Write about:

- what characters say and do that shows society is divided
- how Russell presents a divided society by the way he writes.

[30 marks]

[SPaG 4 marks]

Edexcel

Your response will be marked for a range of appropriate vocabulary and sentence structures, and for accurate use of spelling and punctuation.

Mickey: Well, how come you got everything ... an' I got nothin'? (*Pause*)

Explore the importance of social division in *Blood Brothers*.

You **must** refer to the context of the play in your answer.

[Total for question = 40 marks (includes 8 marks for using a range of appropriate vocabulary and sentence structures, and for accurate use of spelling and punctuation)]

WJEC Eduqas

You should use the extract and your knowledge of the whole play to answer this question.

(See the sample essay on page 87 for an example of a typical extract used in an exam question by WJEC Eduqas.)

Write about the ways in which a divided society is presented throughout the play.

In your response you should:

- refer to the extract and the play as a whole
- show your understanding of the ways a divided society is presented in the play.

[40 marks]

Spot the differences!

- AQA and Edexcel both give a choice of questions to answer.
- Both WJEC Eduqas and AQA direct students to 'write about' and give two bullet points to guide students' responses. WJEC Eduqas also gives a short extract as a stimulus for students.

- Edexcel states explicitly the need to refer to the 'context' of the play.
- Only Edexcel does not assess AO2 in this section.
- Only WJEC Eduqas does not assess AO3 in this section.
- The questions from AQA are marked out of 34 (up to 30 marks for your answer and up to 4 marks for SPaG). The questions from Edexcel are marked out of 40 (up to 32 marks for your answer and up to 8 marks for SPaG). The question from WJEC Eduqas is marked out of 40.

Approaching the AQA and Edexcel questions

Before choosing your question, read them both carefully and make sure you understand exactly what the tasks require you to do. Think very carefully before deciding which question to attempt. Choose the question that gives you the best chance to impress the examiner with your depth of knowledge.

Approaching the WJEC Eduqas question

First, read the extract very carefully, trying to get an overview or general impression of what is going on, and what or who is being described.

Now read the extract again, underlining or highlighting any words or short phrases that you think are relevant to the focus of the question and of special interest. For example, they might be surprising, unusual or amusing. You might have a strong emotional or analytical reaction to them or you might think that they are particularly clever or noteworthy.

These words/phrases may work together to produce a particular effect, or to get you to think about a particular theme, or to explore the methods the writer uses to present a character in a particular way for their own purposes.

You may pick out examples of literary techniques such as use of imagery or contrast, or sound effects such as alliteration, or a particularly clever use of stagecraft. You may spot an unusual word order, sentence construction or use of punctuation. Don't forget to consider the effect of stage directions, if included, as well as dialogue. The important thing to remember is that when you start writing you must try to *explain the effects* created by these words/phrases or techniques, and not simply identify what they mean. Above all, ensure that you are answering the question.

Planning your answer

For all exam boards, it is advisable to write a brief plan before you start writing your response to avoid repeating yourself or getting in a muddle. A plan is not a first draft. You will not have time to do this. In fact, if your plan consists of any full sentences at all, you are probably eating into the time you have available for writing a really insightful and considered answer.

A plan is important, however, because it helps you to gather and organise your thoughts, but it should consist only of brief words and phrases.

You may find it helpful to use a diagram of some sort – perhaps a spider diagram. This may help you keep your mind open to new ideas as you plan, so that you can slot them in. Arranging your thoughts is then a simple matter of numbering the branches in the best possible order. Or you could make a flow chart or list instead. The important thing is to choose a method that works for *you*.

The other advantage of having a plan is that if you run out of time, the examiner can look at the plan and may be able to give you an extra mark or two based on what you were about to do next.

Writing your answer

Now you are ready to start writing your answer. The first thing to remember is that you are working against the clock and so it's really important to use your time wisely.

It is possible that you may not have time to deal with all the points you wish to make in your response. If you simply identify several language features and make a brief comment on each, you will be working at a fairly low level. The idea is to select the ones that you find most interesting and develop them in a sustained and detailed manner. In order to move up the levels in the mark scheme, it is important to write a lot about a little, rather than a little about a lot.

Part of exam technique is making sure that the examiner knows you are developing an argument. You can make this clear by using 'signal words' to signpost your argument. Above all, ensure that you are answering the question. You must also remember to address the whole question, as you will be penalised if you fail to do so.

GRADE BOOSTER

Avoid beginning your essay by spelling out exactly what you intend to do ('In this essay I will show that…'): just get on with it.

GRADE BOOSTER

Your entire essay builds an argument based on evidence, like a lawyer in court arguing a case, so writing and structuring your essay well and providing evidence is very important.

If you have any time left at the end of the examination, do not waste it! Check carefully that your meaning is clear and that you have done the very best you can. Look back at your plan and check that you have included all your best points. Is there anything else you can add? Keep thinking until you are told to put your pen down!

Referring to the author and title

You can refer to Russell either by name (make sure you spell it correctly) or as 'the writer'. You should never use his first name (Willy) – this sounds as if you know him personally. You can also save time by giving the play title in full the first time you refer to it, and afterwards simply referring to it as 'the play'.

GRADE BOOSTER

Do not lose sight of the author in your essay. Remember that the play is a construct - the characters, their words and their actions have all been created by Russell - so most of your points need to be about what Russell might have been trying to achieve. In explaining how his message is conveyed to you, for instance through an event, something about a character, use of symbolism, personification, irony and so on, don't forget to mention his name. For example:

- Russell makes it clear that…
- It is evident from … that Russell is inviting the reader to consider…
- Here, the reader may well feel that Russell is suggesting…

GRADE BOOSTER

The examiners will expect you to use the appropriate terminology where you can. If you can't decide whether a phrase is a simile or a metaphor, however, it helps just to refer to it as an example of imagery and explain how the author wants the reader to respond to the word-picture he is painting.

Writing in an appropriate style

Remember that you are expected to write in a suitable **register**, meaning you need to use an appropriate style. This means:

- *not* using colloquial language or slang, e.g. 'Sammy is a nasty piece of work. A bit of a toe-rag really.' (The only exception is when quoting directly from the text.)
- *not* becoming too personal, e.g. 'Mickey is like my mate, right, 'cos he...'
- using suitable phrases for an academic essay, e.g. 'It could be argued that...', *not* 'I reckon that...'
- *not* being too dogmatic – don't say 'This means that...'; it is much better to say 'This might suggest that...'.

You are also expected to be able to use a range of technical terms correctly. If you can't remember the correct name for a technique, however, but can describe its effect, you should still go ahead and do so.

The first person ('I')

It is perfectly appropriate to say 'I feel...' or 'I think...'. You *are* being asked for *your* opinion. Just remember that you are being asked for your opinion about *what* Russell may have been trying to convey in his play (his themes and ideas) and *how* he does this (through the characters, events, language, form and structure of the play).

Spelling, punctuation and grammar (AO4)

Your spelling, punctuation and grammar (SPaG) are specifically targeted for assessment on the play, so you cannot afford to forget that you will demonstrate your grasp of the play through the way you write. Take great care with this and don't be careless. If the examiner cannot understand what you are trying to say, they will not be able to give you credit for your ideas.

GRADE BOOSTER

It is important to make the individual quotations you select brief and to try to *embed* them. This will save you time, enabling you to develop your points at greater depth and so raise your grade. To check how good you are at embedding quotations, read your sentences out to someone who has not read the play. See if they can tell where Russell's words begin and end. If they cannot, you have integrated his words smoothly.

How to raise your grade

The most important advice is to answer the question that is in front of you, and to start doing so promptly. When writing essays in other subjects, you may have been taught to write a lengthy, elegant introduction explaining what you are about to do. In the literature examination, though, you have only a short time so it is best to get started as soon as you have gathered your thoughts together and made a brief plan.

Students often ask how long their answer should be. It is difficult to give a definitive answer because clearly candidates have different-sized handwriting and quality is always more important than quantity. A strongly focused answer of 2–3 sides that hits the criteria in the mark scheme is perfectly able to be rewarded at the very highest level. Conversely, if a response is 6–7 sides long but is not focused on the question, it will not receive many marks at all.

Sometimes students go into panic mode because they don't know how to start. It is absolutely fine to begin your response with words from the question itself; in fact this will help you focus your response on the question. For the WJEC Eduqas question you could start with: 'In this extract Russell presents…' because with this exam board you need to refer to the extract. Begin by selecting interesting words and phrases and unpicking or exploring them within the context or focus of the question. For example, if the question is about the way society is presented, you need to focus on picking out words and phrases to do with a divided society.

If you are responding to a more traditional 'essay-style' question (for AQA or Edexcel) it is still important to get quickly to the point. There is no point in simply re-writing the question! If a question asks you to explore the way that class differences are presented in the play, it is perfectly fine to begin: 'Russell uses a variety of methods to explore the significance of class differences in the play.'

Key points to remember

- Do not just jump straight in. Spending time wisely in the first moments may gain you extra marks later.
- Write a brief plan.
- Remember to answer the question.
- Use your time wisely. Try to leave a few minutes to look back over your work and to check your spelling, punctuation and grammar, so that your meaning is clear and so that you know that have done the very best that you can.
- Keep an eye on the clock.

GRADE *FOCUS*

Grade 5

- Candidates have a clear focus on the text and the task and are able to 'read between the lines'.
- Candidates develop a clear understanding of the ways in which writers use language, form and structure to create effects for the readers.
- Candidates use a range of detailed textual evidence to support comments.
- Candidates use understanding of the idea that both writers and readers may be influenced by where, when and why a text is produced.

Grade 8

- Candidates produce a consistently convincing, informed response to a range of meanings and ideas within the text.
- Candidates use ideas that are well linked and often build on one another.
- Candidates dig deep into the text, examining, exploring and evaluating the writer's use of language, form and structure.
- Candidates carefully select finely judged textual references that are well integrated in order to support and develop responses to texts.
- Candidates show perceptive understanding of how contexts shape texts and responses to texts.

Achieving a Grade 9

To reach the very highest level you need to have thought about the play more deeply and produced a response that is conceptualised, critical and exploratory at a deeper level. You might, for instance, challenge accepted critical views in evaluating whether the writer has always been successful. If, for example, you think Russell set out to create sympathy for the working class, how successful do you think he has been?

You need to make original points clearly and succinctly and to convince the examiner that your viewpoint is really your own, and a valid one, with constant and careful reference to the text. This will be aided by the use of short and apposite (really relevant) quotations, skilfully embedded in your answer along the way (see 'Sample essays', page 89).

REVIEW YOUR LEARNING

(Answers are given on page 100.)

1 On which paper is your *Blood Brothers* question?
2 On which section of the paper is your *Blood Brothers* question?
3 Will you be assessed on spelling, punctuation and grammar in your response to *Blood Brothers*?
4 Can you take your copy of the play into the exam?
5 Why is it important to plan your answer?
6 Do you have a choice of questions?
7 Approximately how long do you have to answer the question?
8 What should you do if you finish ahead of time?

Assessment Objectives and skills

All GCSE examinations are pinned to specific areas of learning that the examiners want to be sure candidates have mastered. These are known as Assessment Objectives or AOs. If you are studying *Blood Brothers* as an examination text for AQA, Edexcel or WJEC Eduqas, the examiner marking your exam response will be trying to give you marks, using the particular mark scheme for that board. All mark schemes, however, are based on fulfilling the key AOs for English literature.

Assessment Objectives

The Assessment Objectives that apply to your response to *Blood Brothers* are shown below.

For AQA, Edexcel and WJEC Eduqas:

AO1 Read, understand and respond to texts. Students should be able to:
- maintain a critical style and develop an informed personal response
- use textual references, including quotations, to support and illustrate interpretations.

For AQA and WJEC Eduqas only:

AO2 Analyse the language, form and structure used by a writer to create meanings and effects, using relevant subject terminology where appropriate.

AO2 is *not* assessed on the *Blood Brothers* question if you are entered for the Edexcel examination.

For AQA and Edexcel only:

AO3 Show understanding of the relationship between texts and the contexts in which they were written.

AO3 is *not* assessed on the *Blood Brothers* question if you are entered for the WJEC Eduqas examination.

There is one further AO that applies to all three exam boards that offer *Blood Brothers*:

AO4 Use a range of vocabulary and sentence structures for clarity, purpose and effect, with accurate spelling and punctuation.

What skills do you need to show?

Let's break the Assessment Objectives down to see what they really mean.

AO1 Read, understand and respond to texts. Students should be able to:
- maintain a critical style and develop an informed personal response
- use textual references, including quotations, to support and illustrate interpretations.

At its most basic level, this AO is about having a good grasp of what a text is about and being able to express an opinion about it within the context of the question. For example, if you were to say, 'The play is about the tragedy of twin boys who were separated at birth' you would be beginning to address AO1 because you would have made a **personal response**. An '**informed**' response refers to the basis on which you make that judgement. In other words, you need to show that you know the play well enough to answer the question.

AO1 also requires you to '**use textual references, including quotations, to support and illustrate interpretations**'. This means giving short direct quotations from the text. For example, if you wanted to support the idea that Mickey looks up to Sammy, you could use a direct quote: 'I wish I was our Sammy ... he wees straight through the letter box ... I tried to do it one night'. Alternatively, you can simply refer to details in the text in order to support your views. So you might say, 'Mickey looks up to Sammy and tries to follow his example, as when Sammy urinated through the letter box of the house next door.'

Generally speaking, most candidates find AO1 relatively straightforward. Usually, it is tackled well – if you answer the question you are asked, this Assessment Objective will probably take care of itself.

AO2 Analyse the language, form and structure used by a writer to create meanings and effects, using relevant subject terminology where appropriate.

AO2, however, is a different matter. Most examiners would probably agree that covering AO2 is a weakness for many candidates, particularly those students who only ever talk about the characters as if they were real people.

Remember that AO2 is *not* assessed in this section of the examination if you are entered with Edexcel.

In simple terms, AO2 refers to the writer's methods and is often signposted in questions by the word 'how', e.g. 'How does the writer present…'.

Overall AO2 is equal in importance to AO1 so it is vital that you are fully aware of this objective. The word '**language**' refers to Russell's use of words. Remember that writers choose words very carefully in order to achieve particular effects. They may spend quite a long time deciding between two or three words that are similar in meaning in order to create just the precise effect they are looking for.

If you are addressing AO2 in your response to *Blood Brothers*, you will typically find yourself using Russell's name and exploring the choices he has made. For example, noting that Russell uses the narrator to describe Mrs Johnstone as having 'a stone in place of her heart' will set you on the right path to explaining why this metaphor is an interesting choice. Of course, there is no right or wrong answer to this but you might say not only does it have an idiomatic use, suggesting that someone is cold-hearted, but it also suggests the idea of someone with no feelings or warmth. Even the sound of the word 'stone' is heavy and harsh! It is this explanation that addresses AO2, while 'Mrs Johnstone was cruel' would be a simple AO1 comment.

Language also encompasses a wide range of writer's methods, such as the use of different types of imagery, words that create sound effects, juxtaposition, irony and so on.

AO2 also refers to your use of '**subject terminology**'. This means that you should be able to use terms such as 'metaphor' and 'dialect' with confidence and understanding. Don't despair if you can't remember the term – you will still gain marks for explaining the effects being created!

The terms '**form**' and '**structure**' refer to the kind of text you are studying and how it has been 'put together' by the writer. This might include the narrative technique being used (in *Blood Brothers*, as well as using the characters' own words, Russell also uses a narrator who plays several parts).

The structure of the text is part of the order of events and the effects created by it, and the way key events are juxtaposed. For example, a scene involving the Johnstone family may be followed soon afterwards by a scene in the Lyons' household, thus offering a powerful contrast between working-class and middle-class values. Effects of structure can also be seen in the writer's use of sentence length and order (syntax).

Remember – if you do not address AO2 at all, it will be very difficult to achieve much higher than Grade 1, since you will not be answering the question.

AO3 Show understanding of the relationship between texts and the contexts in which they were written.

This AO, although not perhaps considered as important as AO1 and AO2, is still worth between 15 and 20 per cent of your total mark in the examination as a whole, and so should not be underestimated.

Remember that AO3 is *not* assessed in this section of the examination if you are entered with WJEC Eduqas.

To cover AO3 you must show that you understand the links between a text and when, why and for whom it was written. For example, some awareness of how the working classes were treated in the 1980s may well help you to understand Russell's intentions in writing *Blood Brothers* to help change the attitudes of a largely middle-class audience. Equally, some knowledge of Russell's background might give you useful insight into his concern about the treatment of the working classes in the 1980s. *Blood Brothers* was written at a time of high unemployment and of an attitude that there was no such thing as society, only individuals who could achieve whatever they wanted through their own efforts.

It is important to understand, however, that context should not be 'bolted on' to your response for no good reason; you are writing about literature not history!

AO4 Use a range of vocabulary and sentence structures for clarity, purpose and effect, with accurate spelling and punctuation.

This AO is fairly self-explanatory. It is worth remembering that it is assessed in your response to *Blood Brothers* and that a clear and well-written response should always be your aim. If your spelling is so bad or your grammar and lack of punctuation so confusing that the examiner cannot understand what you are trying to express, this will obviously adversely affect your mark!

Similarly, although there are no marks awarded for good handwriting, and none taken away for untidiness or crossings-out, it is obviously important for the examiner to be able to read what you have written. If you believe your handwriting is so illegible that it may cause difficulties for the examiner, you need to speak to your school's examination officer in plenty of time before the exam. They may be able to arrange for you to have a scribe or to sit your examination using a computer.

What you will *not* gain many marks for

You will **not** gain many marks if you do the following:

- **Retell the story.** You can be sure that the examiner marking your response knows the text inside out. You will, at times, have to refer to a certain point in the play, but that should be focused and brief. A key feature of the lowest grades is 'retelling the story'. Don't do it.
- **Quote long passages.** Remember, the point is that every reference and piece of quotation must serve a very specific point you are making. If you quote at length, the examiner will have to guess which bit of the quotation you mean to serve your point. Don't impose work on the examiner – be explicit about exactly which words you have found specific meaning in. Keep quotes short and smart. Remember, this is a closed book examination so you won't have the play with you to refer to.
- **Merely identify literary devices.** You will never gain marks simply for identifying literary devices, such as the use of a simile or rhyme. You *can* gain marks, however, by identifying these features, exploring the reasons you think the author has used them and offering a thoughtful consideration of how they might impact on the reader, as well as giving an evaluation of how effective you think they are.
- **Give unsubstantiated opinions.** The examiner will be keen to give you marks for your opinions, but only if they are supported by reasoned argument and references to the text.
- **Write about characters as if they are real people.** It is important to remember that characters are constructs – the writer is responsible for what the characters do and say. Don't ignore the author!

REVIEW YOUR LEARNING

(Answers are given on page 100.)

1. What does AO1 assess?
2. What sort of material do you need to cover in order to successfully address AO2?
3. What do you understand by the term 'AO3'?
4. Is AO4 assessed on *Blood Brothers*?
5. Which exam board specification are you following and what AOs should you be focusing on?
6. What should you *not* do in your response?

Sample essays

Question 1

The question below is typical of an AQA question and is also similar to an Edexcel question in that you are required to write an essay-type answer.

> The tragic outcome is inevitable from the start. How does Russell present this inevitability in *Blood Brothers*?
>
> Write about:
>
> - how Russell presents the events in the play that lead inevitably to the tragic outcome of the play
> - how Russell uses these events to present his ideas in the play.

You will see below extracts from the exam responses of two students working at different levels. They cover much the same points. If you look carefully, however, you will be able to see how Student Y takes similar material to that of Student X, but develops it further in order to achieve a higher grade.

Student X, who is likely to achieve Grade 5, responds like this:

1 There are no marks for this kind of introduction. At this point the examiner may well be thinking 'Well, get on with it, then.'

I am going to explain how Russell presents the events in the play that lead to the tragic outcome and then explain how Russell uses these events to present his ideas. At the start of the play the Narrator briefly tells the audience what happens and we see the deaths of Mickey and Edward, which tells us that the play has a tragic ending. This makes the audience wonder why they have to die.

2 True. But what is the author's purpose in creating this structure to the play?

Mrs Johnstone is described as being sexier than Marilyn Monroe when she was younger but now as looking much older than her age. She is pregnant again and is surprised to find that she is expecting twins and worried about Social Services taking them away from her. Mrs Lyons, the woman she cleans for, has a solution – she will take one of the twins as she can't have children herself. The Narrator tells us that Mrs Johnstone has a heart of stone but I think Mrs Lyons is really to blame. When Mrs Lyons tells Mrs Johnstone about the superstition that both twins will die if they find out about each other, we know that this will happen because we have seen the final scene at the beginning of the play. This makes it inevitable.

The superstition aspect of the play is emphasised by the Narrator in his song 'Shoes Upon The Table', which is all about superstitions and the fact that 'the devil's got your number', which means that something evil will happen. The kid's games are all about shooting and pretend killings, which foreshadow the real killing of the petrol-station attendant and the twins.

Although both Mrs Johnstone and Mrs Lyons try to keep the twins from seeing each other, the boys become firm friends. This makes it more likely that they will find out that they are twins. Mrs Lyons moves house so that Edward will be away from Mickey but Mrs Johnstone is then rehoused by the council to a place near the Lyons' new house. It seems fated that the boys will meet again. Mrs Lyons certainly thinks so, as she has a mental breakdown and thinks that the only way to save Edward is by stabbing and killing Mrs Johnstone. Russell here shows that the twins' destinies are closely connected, making the outcome of the play inevitable.

The Narrator warns us that, even though Mickey, Edward and Linda are happy during their teenage years, there are bad times ahead. He does this by comparing

3 Showing understanding of the play but tending towards telling the story rather than focusing on the question.

4 Clear understanding shown and a hint of recognition of the writer's methods.

5 Correct use of terminology ('foreshadow').

6 Relevant information and focus on the question.

Linda to lambs in spring who don't know they will be killed soon and illustrates this by having the three of them play 'piggy-in-the-middle' and freezing the action when Linda catches the ball. The Narrator is always interrupting events, commenting on what is happening and reminding the audience that there is a 'price to pay.'

7 Awareness of Russell's methods and their effect on the audience.

8 Nicely embedded quotation.

The writer uses the comparison of Marilyn Monroe's life to Mickey's to foreshadow what will happen to Mickey, thus emphasising the inevitability.

9 Correct, but more detailed explanation needed.

The twins' friendship comes to end when Edward comes back from university and is unable to appreciate Mickey's situation. After Mickey comes out of prison, he is depressed and Linda turns to Edward for help. He does help them but has an affair with Linda. Mrs Lyons tells Mickey about it so we now know that something bad will happen and can see the 'curse' of separated twins coming true. Mickey comes after Edward but doesn't really intend to kill him, but the gun accidently goes off when he is told that Edward is his brother and kills Edward. The police then shoot Mickey so fulfilling the curse that has been inevitable from the beginning of the play.

10 A satisfactory conclusion that refers back to the question.

This response has a promising start that would suggest Student X is working at Grade 5 and is demonstrating 'clear understanding'. The response is focused on the task and there is awareness of Russell's methods and their effects on the audience, though these are not always fully explained. For a higher grade, more detailed explanations of Russell's methods and a greater focus on his ideas would be needed.

A higher-level response to the same question appears next. Student Y is working towards Grade 8. Look carefully and see if you can identify the differences between the two responses.

The concept of inevitability is crucial to a full understanding of Russell's message. Although the twins may be fated to die, Russell is not suggesting that a malignant force is at work, but rather that the nature of society has created conditions that determine the life a person will lead.

1 A strong opening with a clear focus on the question and on the writer's ideas in the play.

The opening of the play makes it clear at once to the audience what will happen – drama and interest are created by Russell posing the question 'why did this happen' – rather than 'what will happen'. This may focus the audience more on Russell's message to them. The play opens with the Narrator summarising the 'story of the Johnstone twins'. This is followed by a re-enactment of the deaths of Mickey and Edward. A sense of foreboding is introduced by the Narrator when he refers to various superstitions, for example that of 'one lone magpie'. This sense of foreboding gradually builds up throughout the play, which emphasises the inevitability.

2 An understanding that this is a play to be performed in front of an audience.

Mrs Lyons manipulates Mrs Johnstone's superstitious nature when she tells her about twins who have been secretly parted dying if they learn that they are 'one of a pair'. As they have already seen the final scene, the audience knows that this will come true, adding to the sense of inevitability that pervades the whole play.

3 Close focus on the question, supported by relevant embedded quotations.

The Narrator has a crucial role to play in creating a sense of the inevitable. He adds a sense of foreboding whenever he appears, often repeating ominous phrases like 'the devil's got your number' to create a sense of inevitable misfortune around the characters. Russell doesn't just have him repeating phrases, however, but builds up the tension in the audience by the Narrator saying how the devil is getting closer and closer – he has been seen staring through the window, then running beside you, to screaming deep inside you and finally he's 'calling your number up today.' By using the metaphor of the devil to represent fate, Russell adds a feeling of evil to the play, making the Narrator a sinister figure. He constantly reminds the audience that there is always a price to pay, a debt to be repaid – the inevitable will happen!

4 Focus on the writer's methods, supported by close reference to the text.

Russell's focus on the importance of society, the individual and the class divide should remind the audience that Russell sees fate not as some sinister force controlling our lives, but rather as how the unjust society we have created affects and dominates our lives. Perhaps the price there is to pay has a deeper relevance – it is not just these two families who have to pay the price for their actions: society itself is also degraded by the class divide it has created.

5 Clear focus on the writer's ideas.

6 An interesting alternative interpretation.

The irony of Mrs Lyons moving house specifically to get away from the Johnstone family – whereas if she had stayed where she was for just a little longer the Johnstone family would have been rehoused away from Mrs Lyons – highlights the sense of inevitability. Nothing Mrs Lyons, or anyone else, can do can prevent the tragic outcome seen enacted at the beginning of the play. Mrs Lyons acts as a catalyst in the play as her guilt and paranoia sets off the train of events that leads to the deaths of the twins, thus fulfilling the superstition about separated twins learning about each other.

By showing the ending at the start, Russell is able to use dramatic irony to reinforce this sense of the inevitable. This is clearly seen when Mickey and Edward first meet – the audience is well aware that these are twins and therefore have no need to become blood brothers to affirm their friendship. The Marilyn Monroe motif employed by Russell, especially when Russell changes it from referring to Mrs Johnstone to linking it with Mickey, is another example of dramatic irony used to foreshadow the ending – the audience would be expected to know of Marilyn Monroe's death and therefore this motif would give rise to a sense of foreboding regarding Mickey's future.

Even in the light-hearted section on 'Kid's games' Russell foreshadows the guns and violence of the end of the play, adding to the inevitability we feel.

The structure of the play also adds to the sense of inevitability. Having no separate scenes to slow down the action, the play moves swiftly and inexorably towards its tragic climax.

The play comes swiftly to its conclusion once Mickey learns from Mrs Lyons about the relationship between Edward and Linda. Whether it is only a 'light romance' or a proper affair, the audience knows now how the play will reach its predestined tragedy. I think, however, that to make sure he gets his message across to the audience, Russell has the Narrator pose the question to the audience: is superstition or our class system to blame for what has happened? He clearly invites us to blame society and not fate for these inevitable events.

7 Clear focus on the writer's methods, closely related to the question.

8 An effective conclusion, focusing on both Russell's methods and ideas, and linking back to the question.

Question 2

The sample responses below are based on the following WJEC Eduqas-style question, which focuses on character rather than theme. A given extract from the play is provided as a stimulus and then the response is required to widen out and consider the character(s) in the play as a whole. The extract for this question is from pages 8 to 9, from when Mrs Lyons says 'Actually, Mrs J' to when Mrs Lyons exits with the shoes.

> You should use the extract and your knowledge of the whole play to answer this question.
>
> Write about how Russell presents the relationship between Mrs Johnstone and Mrs Lyons.
>
> In your response you should:
>
> - refer to the extract and to the play as a whole
> - show your understanding of characters and events in the play.
>
> [Total for question = 40 marks (includes 5 marks for accuracy in spelling, punctuation and vocabulary/sentence structures)]

Student X, who is aiming for a Grade 5, begins his or her response like this:

> In the passage Mrs Lyons and Mrs Johnstone are talking about having babies. Mrs Lyons can't have children but Mrs Johnstone 'can't stop havin' them'. She reassures Mrs Lyons that she will be able to continue cleaning for her. Right from the start Russell contrasts the two women by the way they speak. Mrs Johnstone uses slang terms like 'kids' but Mrs Lyons is more formal and talks about 'children', which shows the audience that Mrs Lyons is from a higher class. Mrs Johnstone is shocked when she sees Mrs Lyons putting a pair of new shoes on the table. This is a bad omen according to Mrs Johnstone, who is very superstitious. Mrs Lyons takes the shoes away to keep Mrs Johnstone happy. Both characters seem to like each other at this

1 Support from the extract but fails to comment on what the difference in language use between Mrs Johnstone and Mrs Lyons tells us about them.

2 Tending to write about what happens in the extract rather than focusing on the question; a common error with questions containing an extract from the text.

3 Clear understanding of the writer's method but little explanation.

point in the play, but their feelings towards each other change as the play progresses. When she finds that Mrs Johnstone is expecting twins, Mrs Lyons has the idea of taking one of them. She can't have children herself and Mrs Johnstone is worried about being able to feed two more mouths. Mrs Johnstone can see a better future for one of the twins if he is raised by Mrs Lyons, who is comfortably well-off and could give a child everything he would need. Mrs Lyons takes advantage of Mrs Johnstone's superstitious and simple nature by getting her to agree to give up one of the babies by swearing on the Bible.

Mrs Johnstone is presented as very maternal and as loving all her children. Once the twins have been born, Mrs Johnstone seems to have second thoughts about giving up one of them. She realises that, like the goods she buys on the never never, one of the babies is only hers until it's time 'to pay the bill'. She asks Mrs Lyons if she could keep them for a few more days but Mrs Lyons is determined to get one of babies immediately, showing she has power over Mrs Johnstone. When Mrs Lyons sacks Mrs Johnstone, she makes sure Mrs Johnstone doesn't tell anyone about the baby by threatening her with the superstition that both twins will die if they ever find out about the other's existence. Russell shows a nasty side to Mrs Lyons here, which becomes even worse when she goes mad and tries to stab Mrs Johnstone because she thinks Mrs Johnstone is deliberately following her around and becomes frightened the twins will find out that they are 'one of a pair' and die.

4 Some appreciation of the writer's methods although not explicitly stated.

5 Appropriate, if general, comment on character.

Now compare how Student Y, who is working at Grade 8, begins his or her response to the same question. Look carefully and see if you can identify the differences between the two responses.

In this extract Russell presents us with two women who are in sharp contrast with each other. Whereas Mrs Lyons is wealthy, middle-class and without children, Mrs Johnstone is from poor working-class background and has had seven children, with two more on the way. Their different backgrounds are immediately obvious from the language they use. Mrs Johnstone's Liverpudlian slang and down-to-earth language – 'me husband used to say that all we had to do was shake hands and I'd be in the club.' – is in stark contrast to Mrs Lyons' refined Standard English ('We've been trying for such a long time now'). Their difference in language use also defines their relationship: Mrs Lyons, as Mrs Johnstone's employer, is in a position of power and can dominate Mrs Johnstone. So, although they are on friendly terms in this extract, it is not a friendship of equals.

It is at this point that the important theme of superstition is introduced, when Mrs Lyons places the new shoes on the table. The fact that Russell describes Mrs Johnstone as being so 'relieved' when Mrs Lyons humours her by removing the shoes reveals the extent of Mrs Johnstone's superstitious nature. Later on Mrs Lyons is able to use her superstitious nature against her when she insists on a binding agreement by getting Mrs Johnstone to lay her hand on the Bible. Mrs Johnstone's motives for giving up one of her children are clearly shown to be for the child's best interests, as the duet 'My Child' between the two women reveals

1 Immediate focus on the extract and the writer's method.

2 Focus on how Russell defines their relationship through language.

(a duet is an appropriate vehicle for the song as it signifies their agreement). It can be argued of course that Mrs Johnstone makes the right decision as Russell shows Edward achieving in life, unlike Mickey. This song would make the audience question the Narrator's metaphorical comment at the beginning of the play that Mrs Johnstone had 'a stone in place of her heart.' This reference to the stone-hearted woman fits more easily on Mrs Lyons when she sacks Mrs Johnstone on the pretence that her work has deteriorated, thus denying her access to her own child – which was part of the original agreement.

More significantly, however, Mrs Lyons is able to manipulate Mrs Johnstone's superstitious nature to threaten her to keep quiet by saying how both twins will die if they find out about the other and if Mrs Johnstone does reveal the secret she will be responsible for their deaths. As the audience has seen a re-enactment of the final scene, this becomes not so much a warning as a prophecy. Is this a known curse or is Mrs Lyons being devious and just making it up to terrify Mrs Johnstone? In view of later events between the two, especially Mrs Lyons' attempt on Mrs Johnstone's life, I would suggest the latter explanation is the more likely.

3 An interesting idea advanced.

4 Detailed understanding of the text.

5 Awareness of an audience and insight into the play's structure.

6 Beginning to explore character and ideas.

Student X continues as follows:

Mrs Lyons feels guilty about having Edward and so she becomes over-protective of him, not allowing him out to play and calling her husband home from work when Edward is missing for a short time. Mrs Johnstone has a more care-free attitude to her children and although Sammy has to have a metal plate in his head because he fell out of a window, it was not Mrs Johnstone's fault as she had to go to work.

The final meeting between Mrs Lyons and Mrs Johnstone shows that Mrs Lyons has gone mad. She thinks that Mrs Johnstone is deliberately following her and therefore the twins will find out that they 'was once a pair' and will die. In her madness, she tries to stab Mrs Johnstone but fails. Funnily enough, she is the one who tells Mickey about Linda and Edward and so accidently brings about their deaths, something she has been trying to avoid.

Russell mainly presents her character through the use of song, in which she is compared to Marilyn Monroe, a glamorous Hollywood star. She is said to have been sexier than Marilyn Monroe but then her husband left her for a younger woman as Mrs Johnstone became twice the size of Marilyn and his new partner looked a little like Marilyn Monroe.

1 Good comparison between the two women.

2 Aware of the irony but fails to use correct terminology.

3 Some insight shown.

4 Awareness of the writer's method, but more descriptive than analytical.

Student Y continues as follows:

Russell continues to present the characters of these two 'mothers' through contrast. Mrs Johnstone has a strong maternal love for her children, loving them all intensely, although her circumstances may prevent us describing her as a 'good' mother. After all, Sammy nearly dies from falling out of an upstairs window and she has a tendency to blame others for her children's misbehaviour – for example when Sammy burns the school down. She is very down-to-earth and can relate easily to teenagers (e.g. when Mickey and Edward want to go to the pictures). Although aware of her failings as a mother (as she says to Mickey '...you've not had much of a life with me, have y'?'), she is very supportive of her children and has a warm-hearted and generous nature. While Mrs Lyons also loves Edward, this love becomes possessive, over-protective and stifling, leading to her paranoia and mental breakdown when she thinks Mrs Johnstone is following her and that the only way to stop her is by killing her! Ironically, it is this over-protectiveness and guilt that leads to the death of the twins, something she has spent her life trying to prevent. As she states, 'I took him. But I never made him mine.' Ironically, she appears to have come to believe her own warning. It is her pointing out to Mickey the relationship that Edward has started with Linda that quickly leads to the tragic final scene of the play.

Russell uses the important motifs of Marilyn Monroe and dancing to represent the glamour of Mrs Johnstone in her youth, but also to add a sense of foreboding to the play as an audience would be expected to know of Marilyn Monroe's tragic fate.

1 Detailed exploration of character.

2 Understanding of Russell's use of irony.

3 Commenting on the writer's method and effect.

Student X concludes as follows:

> *Russell shows the difference in class between Mrs Johnstone and Mrs Lyons and how this affects the way they live their lives and the chances they each have in life.*

1 A very brief conclusion containing some comment on Russell's ideas.

Student Y ends his or her response like this:

> *In conclusion, I think that Russell uses Mrs Johnstone as a means to explore the nature vs nurture debate, highlighting the effect of environmental factors on an individual's life. The contrast Russell creates between Mrs Johnstone and Mrs Lyons, in their use of language and financial and social standing, is an ideal means to portray his message about how class divide creates an unjust society.*

1 A fuller conclusion, which addresses more of Russell's ideas and use of methods in the play.

Overall, Student X has produced an answer showing some clear and sustained understanding of the text. The response is much stronger on AO1 than on AO2, which might suggest that this student only just achieves a mark at the lower end of Grade 5. More detailed analysis of the writer's methods and ideas would improve the response.

Student Y has produced a convincing and thoughtful response that offers a range of interpretations and begins to explore various aspects of the play, including the writer's methods and ideas. Russell's use of language and its effects are closely analysed and there is strong effective support, both from the extract and from outside of it, indicating a detailed knowledge of the play.

Top quotations

As your examination will be 'closed book' (you are not allowed to take the text into the exam with you), you might find it helpful to memorise some quotations to use in support of your points in the examination response. If you are unsure which exam board will be setting your question, check with your teacher or see page 67 in the 'Tackling the exams' section.

In this section you will find quotations relating to the main characters and themes of the play, as well as an indication of why each quotation is important.

GRADE BOOSTER

The most frequently used method for learning quotations is to write them down, repeat them and then test yourself. If you are a visual learner, however, you might try drawing an image of one of these quotes with the quotation as a caption.

Top character quotations

The following quotations can be used as a quick reminder of the way that Russell presents the key characteristics of each of the main characters.

Mrs Johnstone

1 'He told me I was sexier than Marilyn Monroe ... we went dancing ... No more dancing' (pages 5–6)

- The dancing motif symbolises the good and the bad times for Mrs Johnstone and also links in with the Marilyn Monroe motif that is used throughout the play.

2 'By the time I was twenty-five / I looked like forty-two' (page 6)

- These lines illustrate the effect that poverty and seven children has had on her – and why her husband left her for a younger woman, who looked 'a bit like Marilyn Monroe'.

3 '...you never put new shoes on the table.' (page 9)

- The first example in the play of Mrs Johnstone's superstitious nature.

GRADE BOOSTER

If you can't remember a full quotation, try and recall its main message. For example, in quotation 2, you could state that after having so many children Mrs Johnstone looked much older than she actually was. This close reference could help you to explain how Russell is suggesting that living in poverty is detrimental to the health of working-class people.

Mrs Lyons

'Wherever I go you'll be just behind me. I know that now ...' (page 78) 4

- Spoken just before she attempts to stab Mrs Johnstone, this utterance reveals both her guilt and her complete mental breakdown.

Mickey

'...how come you got everything ... an' I got nothin'?' (page 105) 5

- Mickey's realisation that society has made life so unfair to him and so advantageous to Edward.

'I could have been ... I could have been him!' (page 106) 6

- Perhaps Mickey's most important utterance in the play, summing up Russell's message.

Edward

'I've always loved you, you must have known that.' (page 93) 7

- Edward's declaration of love for Linda, coming too late as she has married Mickey.

Narrator

'And do we blame superstition for what came to pass? / Or could it be what we, the English, have come to know as class?' (page 107) 8

- The fundamental question being asked by Russell in the play: nature or nurture?

GRADE BOOSTER

Another useful method is to record quotations on to your mp3 player and play them over and over. Or you might try watching extracts on YouTube and spotting where a quotation appears. This can be an effective method as you have both sound and vision to help you, and you can see the quotation in context.

Top theme quotations

1 '**Narrator**: Yes, y' know the devil's got your number' (page 24)

- Reminding the audience of fate and inevitability.

2 '**Mrs Johnstone**: I've spent all me bleedin' life knowin' I *shouldn't*. But I do. Now, take y' soddin' wireless and get off' (page 17)

- A humorous slant on the poverty that afflicts the Johnstone family, but also revealing some self-awareness by Mrs Johnstone.

3 '**Mickey**: You! Why didn't you give me away?' (page 106)

- Mickey's realisation of Edward's privileged life; how nurture (society and the class system) has been good to Edward but not to Mickey.

4 '**Edward**: You might as well know, if I'm not going to see you again. I've always loved you, you must have known that.' (page 93)

- Edward's declaration of love for Linda, coming too late.

GRADE BOOSTER

The memory part of your brain loves colour! Try copying these quotes out using different colours for different characters. You might organise them into mind maps or write them on to sticky notes and put them up around your room. Flash cards can also be fun and effective if you can enlist the help of a partner.

Wider reading

Russell's works (selected)

- *Keep Your Eyes Down* (play, 1972)
- *Our Day Out* (play, 1977; made-for-TV film, 1976; adapted for musical, 1983)
- *John, Paul, George, Ringo ... and Bert* (musical, 1974)
- *Educating Rita* (play, 1980; film, 1983)
- *Shirley Valentine* (play, 1986; film, 1989)
- *Our Day Out – The Musical* (2009/10)

Other fiction linked by theme to *Blood Brothers*

- *The Corsican Brothers* by Alexandre Dumas, père – a novella written in 1844, thought to be the basis for *Blood Brothers* although Russell has denied this influence.
- *Billy Elliot* – a film set during the 1984–85 coal miners' strike; part of the film contains a realistic portrait of the struggles of working-class families at that time of unrest. Turned into a novel (of the same name) by Melvin Burgess in 2001.
- *Wuthering Heights* by Emily Brontë – a classic of English literature; an underlying theme of nature vs nurture can be discerned in this Victorian Gothic novel.
- *I Know This Much Is True* by Wally Lamb – a story about twins, one with a mental illness.

Real-life stories about twins separated at birth

- *Identical Strangers: A Memoir of Twins Separated and Reunited* by Elyse Schein and Paula Bernstein
- *Separated @ Birth: A True Love Story of Twin Sisters Reunited* by Anais Bordier and Samantha Futerman

Websites you may find useful

- www.telegraph.co.uk/culture/theatre/9605796/Willy-Russell-I-want-to-talk-about-things-that-matter.html — an article in the *Daily Telegraph*, covering Russell's life and works, including an interview with the author.
- www.willyrussell.com — a website containing a wealth of information on the author and his works.
- www.funtrivia.com/en/Humanities/Blood-Brothers-13155.html — 65 quick fun and factual questions on *Blood Brothers* (very useful for revision).

Answers

Answers to the 'Review your learning' sections.

Context (p. 14)

1. Willy Russell was born in 1947 near Liverpool.
2. Increased poverty, rising crime, areas became run-down, illegal drug use.
3. The Beatles.
4. Using Marilyn Monroe as a symbol; children's games based on cowboy and gangster films.
5. How much a person's life is determined by their inherited genes and how much is determined by the environment they grow up in.

Plot and structure (p. 25)

1. It allows the play to move swiftly and smoothly to its inevitable conclusion.
2. Seventeen years. The stage directions are more vague: she looks as if she was fifty although she is only thirty years old.
3. She is employed by Mrs Lyons to do the cleaning.
4. She is shocked when she sees Mrs Lyons put new shoes on the table.
5. She tells them that he has died and gone to heaven to be with Jesus.
6. Cowboys and Indians; gangsters; cops and robbers.
7. Threatens him with a knife and tries to steal his money.
8. For example the fairground, beach and chip shop.
9. For example commenting on the action.
10. Superstition or the class system.

Characterisation (p. 41)

1. By what characters say and how they say it; by what characters do; by what others say about them; through stage directions and other forms of stagecraft.
2. For example maternal, superstitious and generous for Mrs Johnstone. She has had many children and loves them all but has a gullible side to her nature that makes her easily manipulated by Mrs Lyons.
   For example unfulfilled, over-protective and manipulative for Mrs Lyons. She is lonely as she is desperate to have children but cannot. Once she has Edward her guilt makes her paranoid about his safety. She sees how superstitious Mrs Johnstone is and easily manipulates her into giving up one of the twins.

3 His teenage years.
4 He speaks in Standard English while Mickey speaks with a Liverpudlian accent; he is generous with his sweets while Mickey is suspicious; he has led a sheltered life while Mickey is street-wise and knows lots of rude words.
5 She protects and mothers him.
6 Out of loyalty to Mickey, his blood brother.
7 For example milkman, bus conductor, Edward's teacher, Mickey's teacher, rifle range man.
8 For example policeman, judge, gynaecologist.
9 Disaffected youth at the time the play was set.
10 Capitalism.

Themes (p. 56)

1 An expression of the writer's key ideas.
2 For example social class and how society shapes people's lives, and the nature vs nurture issue and class divide.
3 As they have the same genes, the way their lives develop can be due only to environmental factors (nurture).
4 When the twins first meet, aged seven.
5 Mrs Lyons putting new shoes on the table. Four other superstitions: for example killing a spider, breaking a mirror, spilling salt, walking on pavement cracks.
6 It is not a malignant force that controls our lives, it is the society we have created.
7 His education is irrelevant to his needs.
8 A recurring idea that reinforces a theme.
9 It helps place the play in its historical context; it emphasises the glamour of Mrs Johnstone in her youth; it contrasts the glamour of Hollywood with the poverty of the Johnstone family; it parallels the fortunes of the Johnstone family.
10 Guns, games and dancing.

Language, style and analysis (p. 66)

1 To highlight the theme of class divide.
2 Simile.
3 They help to convey the author's ideas.
4 To help the play flow smoothly with no cumbersome scene changes.
5 A method by which the author hints at what is to come, indicating beforehand what will happen.

6 For example when Sammy, as a boy, says he is going to get a real gun.
7 For example to express emotion; to create atmosphere; to remind the audience of the key themes of the play.
8 Pathetic fallacy.
9 Links the play with traditional fairy tales, reminding the audience that this is just a story.
10 When a character says or does something and is unaware of its importance, but the audience understands its relevance. Two examples: when Mickey and Edward first meet and don't realise that they are twins; when Mrs Lyons thinks an adopted child can become her own without any explanation.

Tackling the exams (p. 75)

1 AQA and WJEC Eduqas: Paper 2.
Edexcel: Paper 1.
2 AQA and WJEC Eduqas: Section A.
Edexcel: Section B.
3 Yes.
4 No.
5 It helps you to organise your thoughts.
6 AQA and Edexcel: yes.
WJEC Eduqas: no.
7 AQA: approximately 40–45 minutes.
Edexcel: approximately 50 minutes.
WJEC Eduqas: approximately 45–50 minutes.
8 Check your meaning is clear; check you haven't missed any important points; check your spelling, punctuation and grammar.

Assessment Objectives and skills (p. 80)

1 Your ability to read, understand and respond to texts.
2 Analyse the language, form and structure used by a writer.
3 Show understanding between texts and the contexts in which they were written.
4 Yes.
5 If you don't know, ask your teacher. Check page 67 in the 'Tackling the exams' section for the AOs you need to focus on. (All boards assess AO1 and AO4.)
6 Don't: retell the story; use long quotations; only identify literary devices; give unsupported opinions; write about characters as if they were real people.

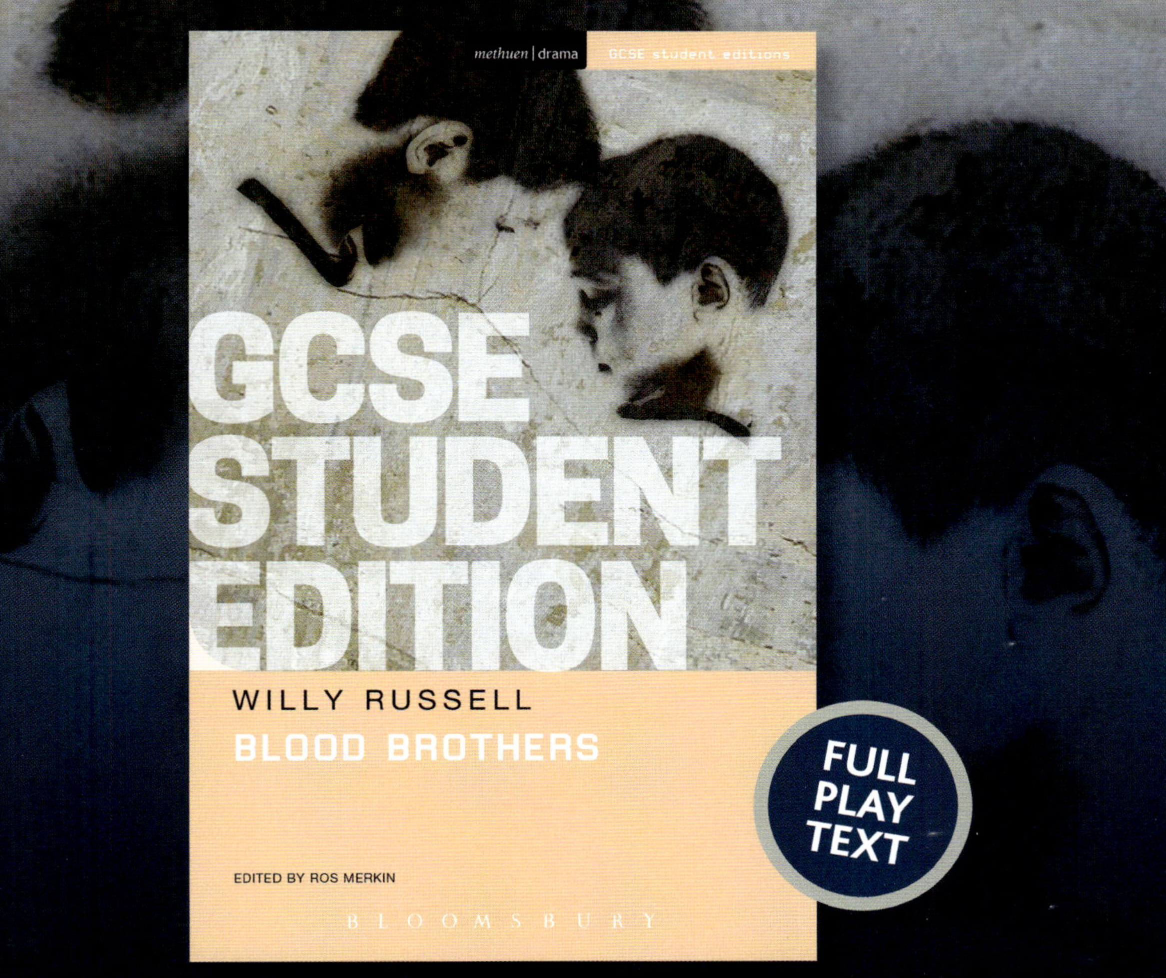
methuen | drama
GCSE student editions
GCSE STUDENT EDITION
WILLY RUSSELL
BLOOD BROTHERS
FULL PLAY TEXT
EDITED BY ROS MERKIN
BLOOMSBURY